The Alphabet of

The Alphabet of Paradise

An A–Z of Spirituality for Everyday Life

HOWARD COOPER

Walking Together, Finding the Way
SKYLIGHT PATHS® Publishing
Woodstock, Vermont

Alphabet of Paradise:
An A–Z of Spirituality for Everyday Life

© 2003 Howard Cooper

Published and distributed in the United States and Canada by
SkyLight Paths Publishing

Originally published in 2002 in Great Britain by
Darton, Longman and Todd Ltd

Library of Congress Cataloging-in-Publication Data

Cooper, Howard, 1953–
The alphabet of paradise : an a–z of spirituality for everyday life / Howard
   Cooper.
      p. cm.
Includes bibliographical references.
ISBN 1-893361-80-2
1. Spiritual life.   2. Spiritual life—Judaism.   3. Self-actualization
   (Psychology)—Religious aspects.   I. Title.
BL624.C6643   2003
291.4'4—dc21

                                                              2002014996

10 9 8 7 6 5 4 3 2 1

Manufactured in Great Britain

SkyLight Paths Publishing is creating a place where people of different
spiritual traditions come together for challenge and inspiration, a place
where we can help each other understand the mystery that lies at the
heart of our existence.
SkyLight Paths sees both believers and seekers as a community that
increasingly transcends traditional boundaries of religion and
denomination—people wanting to learn from each other, *walking
together, finding the way.*

SkyLight Paths, "Walking Together, Finding the Way" and colophon are
trademarks of LongHill Partners, Inc., registered in the U.S. Patent and
Trademark Office.

Walking Together, Finding the Way
Published by SkyLight Paths Publishing
A Division of LongHill Partners, Inc.
Sunset Farm Offices, Route 4, P.O. Box 237
Woodstock, VT 05091
Tel: (802) 457–4000   Fax: (802) 457–4004
www.skylightpaths.com

For Rafi

Contents

Acknowledgements

I would like to thank the following people, without whom this book would be the poorer: Viv Schuster, for her practical help and thoughtful encouragement; Adam Phillips, for his generosity of spirit and fortifying conversations; my editor at DLT, Brendan Walsh, along with his colleagues, for their enthusiasm for this project; Paul Morrison, for his support and suggestions. Also Professor Howard Jacobs, David Rose, Neville and Margaret Sassienie, Jackie King-Cline, Roberta Harris, Jeremy Eckstein, Trisha Stone, Eva Szita-Morris; and members of the Finchley Reform Synagogue 'Exploring Spirituality' groups. And finally, as ever, my family.

Introduction

What this book is about

'Paradise' is part of the world in which we live, a dimension of everyday life. It is not in some far-off time or place, nor is it beyond death. It is here and now. But how can we experience it day by day, moment by moment? How can we learn to develop our spiritual awareness each day of our lives? In our intimate relationships. When we are on our own (are we not always on our own?). When we are at work. When we are with family or friends. When we meet someone new. When we are in the kitchen. When we are in bed. When we are watching TV or playing sports. When our bodies are tired, or our minds are exhausted, or our feelings are fragmented or numb.

How do we learn to appreciate that paradise is not in some mythical land of the past like the Garden of Eden? Nor is it on some tropical beach in the sun (though it could be if we pay enough attention). Nor is it set in some hoped-for future, a heavenly world, our reward for being good. How can we refine our everyday attentiveness and discover paradise now?

In this book I will take readers on a journey of discovery. Into themselves, into the past (because these questions have been asked for three thousand years), into the discoveries and insights of some who have ventured along this path before us. They do not have all the answers (there are no answers). But they have left us signposts to help us along the way, thoughts which can illuminate our own strivings to live a life filled with meaning, with intensity. Signposts towards paradise.

Why 'paradise'?

The word can be traced back to ancient Greek and Hebrew texts. *Paradisos* and *pardes*. It seems to have been borrowed from the Persians. Originally it meant 'park' or 'enclosure', the places where the kings and nobility relaxed and played. In the Hebrew Bible (the Old Testament) it only appears once, in the love song called The Song of Songs, where it means 'orchard' or 'garden'. Later it was associated with the Garden of Eden. From there it began to be used to describe a state of perfection free from suffering. In Christian thought it became linked to the idea of Heaven. Not necessarily a physical location, more a symbol of an invisible, spiritual world parallel to our own.

In Jewish thought too, 'paradise' mutated from referring to a literal place to being understood as a symbolic dimension of existence interwoven into our own mundane reality. A mental and emotional space inside us all in which we could – with guidance, or luck – experience the mysteries of existence.

In the Jewish mystical tradition – ideas from which are threaded through this book – the word *pardes* took on another, rather daring, symbolic meaning. And it is that meaning which underlies this book's attempt to make spirituality available for everyday life.

PaRDeS

This new meaning of *pardes* grew out of the various ways in which the Hebrew Bible was read and taught. More than two thousand years ago the Bible became the sacred spiritual core of Jewish life. Over many generations there evolved four different approaches to it. The most straightforward was called *P'shat*. This meant the *plain* or literal meaning of a story or text: what do the words in this sentence mean? What is actually happening? Who said what? Where did it happen? What happened next? You can ask these kinds of questions of every verse in the Bible. What is the ordinary, everyday *plain* meaning of these words?

A second approach was called *Remez*. The word literally means hint or allusion. We might think of it as *reminders*. In other words: what does this story we are reading remind you of? What ideas does it conjure up in your mind? What feelings does it generate inside you? What connections do you make between this text and other parts of the Bible – or other parts of your life? What you are reading will suggest things to you, and evoke things in you. It will hint at some wider associations. That is, it will be a *reminder* for you of something else you have read or seen or felt or experienced.

Another approach to the Bible was called *D'rash*. This meant to 'explore imaginatively', to uncover or seek out a *deepening* understanding of the meaning and implications of a story, law or verse. Sometimes it meant finding a deeper ethical or moral meaning inside a text. At other times it meant filling in the gaps in the text, because the Bible can be very concise and doesn't spell out everything that is going on at any one moment. Just like in everyday life, things happen to us, and inside us, that we don't always register fully, or understand at the time. But if we explore our lives and experiences in an imaginative way, we can discover a *deepening* awareness in ourselves that there can be more significance to events than meets the naked eye.

A final approach to texts was called *Sod*. This meant the *secret* or mystical meaning of the Bible's words. It involved reading between the lines for hidden or symbolic meanings. It meant looking with great care and attention at every word, even every letter, of the Bible because all the secrets of the universe were contained within it. And it meant looking at the empty space between the words for new insights into the mystery of life. This approach was followed only by a minority of people, because it was felt to be rather demanding, even dangerous, to try to penetrate into the ultimate mysteries of life and death, the *secret* interconnectedness of everything with everything else.

During the thirteenth century these four approaches to the reading and study of the sacred spiritual texts of the Bible – *P'shat*, *Remez*, *D'rash*, *Sod* – began to be seen by certain mystics as belonging together. They formed an acronym – *P.R.D.S.* – which was pronounced PaRDeS: literally an 'orchard', but symbolising 'paradise'. If you were able to bring together all these different ways of thinking about and experiencing the Bible texts, then you could experience paradise now, here on earth. You would be living in paradise.

It is these four approaches, and variations on them, that I will be using in this book. Whatever the subject-matter of each chapter, this PaRDeS framework will underpin my exploration of how spirituality is part of daily lives. It may be useful to think about this framework using the English equivalents I have found for the Hebrew words: '**P**lain, **R**eminders, **D**eepening, **S**ecret' understanding, a contemporary spirituality to find **Parad**ise now.

How the book is designed

Each of the 26 chapters from A to Z will move through these four levels, though not always in a formal or didactic way. You don't need to worry about working out which level you're on, because it's how they come together to form a whole picture that counts; though you may enjoy the experience of seeing how the layers are woven together to create the unique tapestry of spiritual guidance and illumination which each chapter contains.

The inspiration provided by the four layers of reality will filter through each chapter. I'll share some straightforward, *p*lain thoughts – perhaps everyday practical or personal illustrations of the themes. This will be accompanied by ideas I'm *r*eminded about when I reflect on the subject – these may be biblical, Talmudic, Hasidic or Jewish liturgical motifs, or novels, poems, films etc. Through psychological understandings of the unconscious I will take you *d*eeper into the topic. And finally I will offer you some special or more *s*ecret insights. My aim is to show how, by holding together these various aspects of reality, spirituality is neither an esoteric discipline nor fanciful fantasy, but an important and accessible way of being and living in the world.

Over the past twenty-five years, in my work as a psychotherapist and rabbi, I have found that the creative interplay between these domains of learning can open up wonderful vistas for the human imagination and the human heart. The deep well of Jewish spiritual teachings, which date back to Biblical times; the strand of contemporary psychoanalysis which recognises that to speak of the 'unconscious' is to enter in to territory formerly occupied by religion and spirituality; the inspiration of contemporary novelists, essayists and poets whose work offers spiritual insights into our modern condition: an open-minded engagement with these dimensions of human experience can nurture our spiritual growth and transform our lives.

Who is the book for?

This book is not a simple step-by-step manual or self-help guide. It is not a substitute for close emotional relationships, or material well-being, or physical health, or a good psychotherapist. It's just an attempt to present some complex and elusive ideas about the spiritual dimension to existence in a comprehensible and accessible way.

It's safe to say that this book is unusual. You may be on the margins of a formal religious tradition, or you may have rejected institutional religion as outdated or irrelevant to

5

your everyday concerns. Either way, I hope the PaRDeS approach to spirituality can help you learn to see the spiritual within the everyday world, and to feel and value the spiritual potential within yourself. And not just at odd moments, but as part and parcel of the daily concerns we all face, be it with work, relationships, ill-health, loneliness, or any number of the nameless anxieties and stresses of contemporary living.

And for those of you for whom religion is of importance in your life, I hope this book will add another dimension to your religious life. Spirituality has been a crucial component of all the great religions, although it has sometimes been kept away from 'ordinary' people of faith (particularly women) by religious teachers who were uncomfortable sharing their esoteric knowledge. There may be a place for secrets in life, but Western culture has never been more spiritually lost – nor more in need of guidance from those strands of spiritual wisdom that weren't so available for previous generations.

Suitably translated and transposed into a modern idiom – as this book does – these sources of spiritual richness from the past, combined with newer understandings of what our psyches long for, can feed our soul's yearnings. In our modern world, where temperaments are both easily excited and easily satisfied, the opening up of personal spirituality offers us an antidote to the heady seductions that entice us to immerse ourselves in amusement, indulgence and fun. Not that these are 'bad' qualities – but something in us knows that fullness of life cannot consist of them alone.

How to read this book

The tone of this book is evocative rather than analytical. It is both meditative and opinionated. Because the book takes the reader on a spiritual journey, it would be fruitful to read the chapters chronologically. *The Alphabet of Paradise* might appear to be an A–Z of randomly collected topics. This, however, is only on the surface. There may be wanderings and digressions, but the journey has a shape and a destination.

But the book is also designed to be dipped into at random, according to mood, whim or need. Being systematic in our spiritual lives is not necessarily a virtue. Sometimes it is a chance encounter, a serendipitous happening, an unexpected event, which helps us or inspires us. Sometimes, if we find ourselves attentive enough (this book will speak a lot about attention and how to develop our attentiveness), what we need will arrive at the threshold of our lives. Unplanned for, apparently at random, we will overhear a conversation at the supermarket checkout; meet someone at a party we didn't want to go to; read a magazine article while waiting at the doctor's. And something new will open up in our lives.

We cannot plan for the illumination afforded by 'chance' events – so for some this book will work more like the I Ching. Read non-sequentially it may disrupt the author's idea (my map) of the spiritual itinerary this book contains, but open up your own journey in just the way, and just when, you need it most. We cannot control what life presents us with, but we can develop our attentiveness in order to become more receptive to these moments of personal revelation which are addressed to us alone.

A personal note

The ground had long been prepared during my Manchester childhood. Yet when it happened it came with the force of a revelation. It occurred in a half-empty cinema (now pulled down) on Deansgate in the city centre. Skiving from school one afternoon I went to see Stanley Kubrick's *2001: A Space Odyssey* and found myself transported into another dimension: not so much outer space as inner space. By the end of the film I realised, I *knew*, with all the precocious certainty of a teenager, that there was something else available to us in life other than the material and mundane reality in which we are immersed, something luminous: we could cradle eternity in the palm of our hand. I saw the film three times in that first week it was screened and decided that I no longer wanted to read Law at university, but Religious Studies.

Around this time I met Rabbi Lionel Blue, then at the beginning of an idiosyncratic career that would create its own unique blend of spiritual wisdom and down-to-earth humanity. Over the years I learnt from him how moments of epiphany can occur in the unlikeliest of places – and hardly ever in formal places of worship.

After university I spent time in Israel, immersed in traditional Jewish study and practice. This was a prelude to five years' rabbinical training at the Leo Baeck College in London. But my dissatisfaction with the formal structures of religious observance grew: the essence of spirituality could not be found either in the classroom or any religious insti-tution. I became involved in a Gurdjieff-inspired spiritual community in Scotland, learning how attention to the details of our everyday lives could become a vehicle for spiritual illumination. We could learn to submit to some-thing greater than ourselves, which is yet alive within us, each of us uniquely, individually. The concept of the 'soul' stopped being an idea and became a reality: in myself, and in others.

The search for spiritual understanding took me, via C. G. Jung's depth psychology, into the psychoanalytic com-munity and an appreciation of the profoundly Judaic origins of Freud's approach to our psychological well-being. Having graduated as a Reform rabbi, I trained as a psychotherapist. Since 1980 I have worked in both settings: as a teacher, lecturer, consultant and pastoral leader inside the Jewish community; and as an independent psychoanalytic psychotherapist in private practice. Both these vocations have provided the grounding for my continued interest in and exploration of a spirituality which is integrated into daily life.

Along the way I had many years' involvement with Jewish–Christian and Jewish–Christian–Muslim dialogue conferences, settings where I came to appreciate the common spiritual currency that is shared by these faith communities. Beneath doctrinal differences and differing languages in which these faiths express themselves, there lies a core of mystical teachings which can feed the souls of believers and non-believers alike – if these insights are translated into an everyday and intelligible language.

I learnt that spirituality is not grandiose, flaky or overly complicated (though it can often be presented in a way that obfuscates rather than illuminates) but rooted in the simple mysteries of our emotional, physical and mental lives. The interrelationship between my religious and psychotherapeutic understanding is a continuously fruitful source of insights and discoveries. We are complex human beings whose souls need nurturing. And the ways in which we can nurture and attend to our souls can be both taught and learnt.

Mystically inclined, yet with an emotional need for intellectual coherence, I have been reading about, writing about, thinking about and exploring spirituality – for myself, with individuals, and in groups – for nearly thirty years. I have learned to take it seriously as a dimension of life and learned too that I have a faculty for making it real for others as well. *The Alphabet of Paradise* is a book written in this spirit.

Awe

To see a World in a Grain of Sand
And a Heaven in a Wild Flower,
Hold Infinity in the palm of your hand
And Eternity in an hour.

William Blake

Beginning the journey

William Blake – poet, visionary, mystic philosopher, worldly
failure – wanted to make revolutionaries of us all. He was
awed by the wonders of the everyday and wished us to share
in his vision. He wrote with a preacher's fervour – though
he seems to have hated the formal pieties of conventional
religion – as if all we need to do is open our eyes and look,
and the world would appear unmasked, arrayed in its glory.
We may well wonder: is it that simple? Who would not want
to look around them – in the kitchen, the office, the car, the
supermarket – and sense the wonder of life? Who wouldn't
wish to find mystery, deep meaning, within our grasp and
at every moment?

And yet it feels so elusive, this wonder. We don't seem to
be able to capture awe at will. There may, though, be

moments when we have had an intimation of what Blake is describing. Do you remember those moments? This is the beginning of the journey. *You have known wonder.*

Wonder at the natural world: birdsong, a sunset, a field of wheat in the wind, an eclipse, moonrise. Or maybe it was the sight and smell of a new-born baby. Or a piece of music, or a work of art, or a kiss, or a look across a room – moments when your hair stood on end, your heart pounded, your body registered in one way or another that you were experiencing a moment of wonder, of mystery, of awe (though you may not have thought of it like this). Something larger than you was happening. Something you could not control.

The world is a mystery: a question, not an answer. Perhaps you experienced awe gazing at the stars; or through a photo capturing the huge vastness of the universe, space and time beyond comprehension. And you felt your smallness in the scheme of things. Or a view through a microscope: the world of the infinitely small as astonishing as the world of the infinitely large. We are poised between the boundless universe outside us and the inexhaustible cosmos within us.

And yet I know how hard it is to make room for awe. At this moment we are revolving at 1000 miles per hour, while simultaneously orbiting our nearest star, the sun, at 66,000 miles per hour. The statistics make no sense: they are beyond our minds to comprehend. We remain immersed in our lives – mundane, troubled, complex lives. What help is it to us that the Hubble telescope is transmitting awe-inspiring pictures of stars from the edge of the universe 10–15 billion light years away?

And what does it matter to us, as we breathe in and breathe out at this moment, that the one hundred trillion cells in our bodies are all humming with life? That in each one of them there are tens of thousands of genes coiled on every molecule of DNA? Here we are, at this midpoint between the inexhaustibly large and the infinitesimally small. Scientists now say that the scale between us and the furthest reaches of the universe, and us and the smallest particles of matter, is the same. Remarkably, we stand suspended, midway between everything and next to nothing. Almost as if we are meant to be here, gazing out and gazing in.

Wonder

Look at your hand. Take a close look. The skin, soft and hard and wrinkled and smooth, clear and blotchy, lined and grooved and creviced. The nails, bitten or polished, brittle or firm; the fine hairs, the breathing pores, the warts, the scars, the whorls atop each slender or stubby finger. Those fingerprints, a cliché of a thousand Hollywood movies, but still unique to you. The tendons, the muscles, the blood-vessels, the myriad fine bones beneath the surface. Your hand, so simple, so taken-for-granted. Yet no hand like this has ever existed since creation began. Your own hand, unique – that much overused word, which for once is accurate – that no one has possessed before you, nor ever will again. The mystery of your own hand, its being here now, its being here at all. Is it a cause for wonder? Do you shrug – and what does that shrug mean?

Let the hand stand for you, your existence, inimitable, unprecedented. The mystery of your being here, and not just your body with all its awesome complexity but your mind and feelings in all their majesty and individuality. You who have a particular history, a biography as well as a biology. You who have countless stories and memories and intuitions and desires within you. You are the autobiography of a miracle.

That we are creatures capable of consciousness and speech, of love and joy and self-sacrifice, of courage and compassion, generosity and emotional refinement; that we can endure suffering or dedicate ourselves to caring for others; that we are creatures capable of discriminating between right and wrong, and arguing about what these words mean, and sometimes hating, even murdering, others who think differently to us; that we have all this potential within us, potential that we might use creatively or malignly – reflection on this abundance of being can fill us with that sense of trembling wonderment–bafflement that we call awe.

And we can feel awe too when we think about the evolution of our species and what humankind has discovered it can do with the resources around us and within us. Not only the extraordinary richness and variety of artistic and cultural achievements but also the complexity of scientific and technological creativity: penicillin, microchips, moon-landings, keyhole surgery, fibre-optics, nuclear fission, sky-scrapers. Daily, we depend upon a vast web of interlinked aspects of modernity: electricity, transport, microwaves, sewage systems, computers, communication systems. We have achieved all this. Yet our sense of wonder at it all becomes dulled by familiarity. Then a disaster happens (a train crash), or just an everyday failure or breakdown occurs (the washing machine breaks, a computer virus hits) and with a jolt we are reminded that we have failed to wonder at the sheer magnificence of what the human mind has achieved, at least for us in the Western world.

But what happens when we invoke our creativity and our special place in the scheme of things? Does it sound like special pleading on behalf of the human animal that we are: we who share 98 per cent of our genes with apes, and almost as many with fruitflies and worms? Does it generate awe – or cynicism? Wonder – or sadness? Whatever we make of humanity's achievements and potential, our own particular being, our distinctive unrepeatable self, remains a profound puzzle. We are a mystery to ourselves. We are baffled by the complexity of our physical and emotional and mental life. By the fact that we are, that we exist, that we are conscious, sentient, dreaming, laughing, crying, playful beings. And that we are the most destructive creatures in existence.

Wisdom

Our spiritual journey begins with awe. For *awe is the beginning of wisdom*. This is not a new insight. Almost three and a half thousand years ago an anonymous Hebrew poet, somewhere in Babylon or Palestine, collected together a book of wisdom, of maxims and quips and sayings for everyday use. This poet-philosopher, cloaking himself in the authority of the archetypal wise man King Solomon, has one refrain running through his teachings: '*Awe of the Eternal* is the beginning of knowledge ... the beginning of wisdom is one's *awe at the Eternal ... awe at Eternity* is a lesson in wisdom' (Proverbs 1:7, 9:10, 15:33).

What's the meaning of this Hebrew phrase – *yirat Adonai* – which occurs over and again? The Hebrew word for awe contains (as does the English) the sense of both 'wonder' and 'fear'. How can one word seem to point in opposite directions? We can grasp this paradox about awe from our own experiences. When I reflect with wonder at human achievements such as splitting the atom, I also tremble at the destructive potential such extraordinary feats can unleash. Many people have misgivings about unregulated experimentation with genetic engineering or biochemical technology; their anxiety illustrates that our wonder at how scientific progress has aided humanity's progress is balanced by our fears about how such creativity could also lead to harm. And when planes laden with fuel can turn from an integral part of our civilisation's transport system into a weapon of terror, we are poised on the boundary between wonder and fear.

Is awe always a mixed emotion? Does it always have a tension within it between a sense of wonder and a fear for the fragility of life? Maybe. Think of the other side of our wonder at nature. We can enjoy natural history programmes revealing to us the wonders of the deep – but oceans may also drown us. Sunsets fade (like lives). Babies can fall ill, and die. Nature is amoral – we may gaze at mountain peaks while knowing that they unleash avalanches which can snap us in two like a twig.

And when we turn from the doublesidedness of the natural world to our own human nature, awed wonder at what the human mind can encompass within itself can dissolve into fearful awe at the mind's self-evacuation during the ravages of Alzheimer's disease. Awe is not a sentimental emotion. Perhaps it isn't even an emotion at all. Perhaps it's more a state of mind, one in which we hold together our innate sense of wonder with our awareness of the fragility and finitude of all matter (including ourselves). Is this why awe leads to wisdom – because it introduces us to humility and a sense of perspective?

If we look again at the Hebrew, we see we're being pointed towards a mystery. And the mystery is rooted in the second word of this recurring phrase: *Adonai* – Eternity/ the Eternal. In its time this special word for God was a revolutionary breakthrough in our human understanding of how life in the world held together. It was a word made up of four Hebrew letters which formed a strange sound – the exact pronunciation was a secret known only to the initiated few. Nowadays scholars think of it as the word Yahweh, or Jehovah, but this is making a specific name out of a word which blended together the past, present and future tenses of a *verb*. The verb 'to be'. In other words, the God-word invented by the Hebrew people in the course of their history was a term which meant 'being', 'being-and-becoming', 'was-is-will be', 'that which is in the process of unfolding'. Often this was thought of in a personalised way, as if 'God' was a powerful parent: 'the One who was, is and will be', 'the Eternal One'. At other times 'God' was understood in a less personal, more abstract way: 'that which is Eternal'.

It is important to understand the Bible's special name for the divine if we are to appreciate some of the ideas within this book. Spirituality is very much an adventure in extending our awareness of 'that which is', at every moment and in every place. This is so powerful and potentially overwhelming (and subversive) an idea that in the past religious leaders felt the need to teach that God was a personality. This both protected people from the awesome nature of Being, and limited 'God' into a mental shape that could be controlled (unlike life itself). Sadly, *Adonai* became a noun rather than a verb. 'God' became a thing, rather than a process. To be in awe of what is and could be is a very different state of mind from living 'in fear of the Lord' (which is how the phrase is normally translated).

Our translations determine our thinking. When I hear that '*wonder at Eternity* is the beginning of wisdom' I experience a frisson of excitement and challenge far removed from what happens when I read that '*the fear of the Lord* is the beginning of wisdom'. I begin to see that a pathway exists between how I experience everyday life, and my potential for a deeper experience of that life. And that within that journey there's the possibility of a blossoming in my understanding of how things are. This enriched understanding is what we once called wisdom.

Fresh translations, and fresh understandings of old ideas, can help to liberate us from the confines of conventional thoughts. As William Blake recognised: 'If the doors of perception were cleansed everything would appear to man as it is, infinite.'

Doors of perception

Awe is a natural faculty of the human spirit. But it can be squashed out of us. We may develop a thick carapace of insensitivity, fearfulness, cynicism, or despair which prevents us having the openness to life which can allow us to experience it in all its subtlety and depth (and sometimes horror). Is it possible, we wonder, for our 'doors of perception' to be cleansed? To develop our capacity for awe? Or re-develop it? For we had it once in childhood, before it was mocked or knocked out of us. It may feel too frightening even to ask. We have been disappointed in life so many times that the possibility of changing how we see the world may feel too risky. Can we risk seeing the world anew?

How do we learn, re-learn, to experience awe in everyday life? Can we really pay attention to 'that which is' and discover the infinite in the smallest things in life? Buddhism speaks of how we can develop 'mindfulness' – this refers to the desirability of using attention throughout waking life. Judaism speaks of *kavannah* – attentiveness. Many people feel they need help with this. They seek out a yoga or meditation teacher. Or a therapist – because good psychoanalytic thinking can help develop our capacities for paying attention to what comes into our minds. Some disciplines help you clear your mind; others help you sort out what's on (and in) your mind.

Having a personal guide can be useful, but you can do a lot on your own, learning just to pay attention to what is happening in you – in your thoughts, your feelings, your body – moment by moment. Some people feel it useful to keep a diary or use a sketchbook to help heighten attentiveness. Stopping still at some point in the day, deliberately and knowingly, can also help (see chapter on Quiet). Is there time for some empty space, or does it feel too frightening? Empty space is of course not empty at all, but can we allow ourselves the time to experience what is inside it? This is more difficult than it sounds. The problem of speed, of the pace of life, of the pressures and stresses of the everyday drowns out our attentiveness. 'Doing' becomes compulsive. As if something won't let our bodies and minds stop.

We have to make an effort, sometimes a huge effort, to swim against the tide of one damned thing after another.

To feel in the rush of the passing the stillness of the eternal is easier said than done. We have, and invent, endless distractions. We read when we eat. We eat when we walk down the street, or go to the cinema. We talk while we watch TV. We're cooking while the kids are talking to us. We're planning our futures while ignoring the present. Activities overlap and prevent us being present, being attentive, to what is happening now. Can we stop, even once in the day, and pay attention to the present moment? To other people in their awesome complexity. To the artefacts which surround us, dense with detail. To the natural world, flourishing with a genius all of its own. To ourselves, brimming with hidden life. All of this superabundance – which used to be called the sacred – is what we're given to work with and be with day by day in our desacralised world.

It is helpful not to judge or censor what your attention brings to you, because such habitual responses do block real attentiveness. If we take the task seriously, we can begin to cleanse the doors of our perception and begin to see, or re-see, the Eternal in the everyday. 'The universe is continually communicating itself to us in a cosmic eucharist of waves and particles' writes the novelist Russell Hoban. This is a modern way of expressing an ancient understanding: we are in the presence of something which animates life itself, something other than us which yet flows through us.

In the past religions tried to trap this something, to pin it down, give it names, make it intelligible to the human mind, make us frightened or expectant about its presence. You may be part of a faith tradition which speaks of this Presence, which personalises it (anthropomorphises it), trying to give it a semblance of a human shape or feel, give it human qualities and attributes (love, compassion, anger etc.), trying to make it accessible to our understanding. You may be outside or antagonistic to such traditions. But a sense of awe transcends these traditions. Each of us, whatever our view about religion, has the capacity to experience wonder, and to develop our appreciation of the awesome nature of what life unfolds before us and within us moment by moment. The beauty of the narrative of life on earth.

Bodies

> But O alas, so long, so far
> Our bodies why do we forebear?
> They're ours, though they're not we, we are
> The intelligencies, they the sphere.
>
> *John Donne*

Our bodies, ourselves

John Donne – adventurer, womaniser, member of Parliament, later Dean of St Paul's – wrote the finest love poetry and religious verse of his generation. At the beginning of the seventeenth century, in 'The Extasie', he became the first writer to use the word 'sex' in its modern sense: soul communicates to soul through the desires of the body. But as we read these lines, we still see in them the longstanding Christian antagonism between our bodies and our selves. This dualism, given philosophical weight by Donne's near-contemporary Descartes, says: our bodies are ours but we are not our bodies.

Yet this traditional dichotomy – between body and soul, or body and mind – can be spiritually impoverishing. Is it possible to reconfigure their interrelationship? In this chapter I want to explore the ways in which our bodies are ours, that 'they *are* we, *they* are the intelligencies and *we* the sphere'.

There's a story in the Talmud, the 2000–year-old collection of Judaic homiletic and legal literature, which goes as follows:

Rabbi Akiva said: 'I once followed Rabbi Joshua into a toilet and I learnt three things from him.

'First I learnt that you don't place yourself east-to-west, but north-to-south. Second, I learnt that one doesn't shit standing, but sitting. And thirdly I learnt that one doesn't wipe with the right hand but with the left.'

Ben Azai said to Rabbi Akiva: 'How could you have been so shamelessly insolent towards your teacher?'

Rabbi Akiva replied: 'It is Torah, and I have to learn.'

'It is Torah and I have to learn.' In other words: I have a responsibility to try to understand *Torah*, God's teaching – and one of the ways I can learn about the ways of God is through attentive study of the actions of those who are themselves devoted to studying the ways of God. The Talmud is an extended transgenerational conversation between many different rabbis and teachers, arguing and discussing ethical questions and behavioural issues. Whether this tale is fact or fictional doesn't matter. It is a teaching story and the pedagogic lesson is unambiguous: Rabbi Joshua's physicality, his body and his use of his body, can be a medium for communicating a practical spiritual wisdom – 'It is Torah and I have to learn.'

The Talmud also gives us this scene, in the same self-amused yet instructional vein:

Rabbi Kahana once went and hid under Rav's bed to see how his teacher conducted himself when he had intercourse with his wife. He noted that Rav chatted and joked with her before having sex.

21

Rabbi Kahana said: 'It's as if he's never tasted such good food before!'

'Kahana, are you in here?' said Rav. 'Get out, it's not good manners.'

Rabbi Kahana said: 'It is Torah and I have to learn.'

Perhaps tongue-in-cheek, but Kahana, adopting Akiva's refrain from a previous generation, defends himself from reproof by pointing out that his voyeurism is in fact motivated by his desire to understand God's teaching. And his teacher's sexuality is just as much a part of what Rav has to teach as any words of wisdom he might utter. The body's activity becomes the site of knowledge. And sex is seen as a form of religious activity, a spiritual resource.

Sigmund Freud once wrote to a colleague that 'For various reasons the Jews have undergone a one-sided development and admire brains more than bodies.' Yet these Talmudic stories undermine Freud's stereotype that Jews are more naturally predisposed to the life of the mind rather than the body. Unlike those strands of Christian teaching which, historically, looked askance at the 'pleasures of the flesh' and damned bodily passions as detrimental to human salvation, Judaism rarely split the body from the soul in that way. For Jews – in spite of Woody Allen's caricature of the Jewish intellectual perpetually embarrassed by having to reside in a body – the human body always remained a vehicle for the exploration and celebration of the spiritual.

Devotion in action

The Hasidim were a Jewish mystical revivalist movement that sprung up in eastern Europe in the eighteenth century and captured the hearts and minds of millions. They emphasised a body-based approach to God: singing, dancing, contact with nature, joyful physical movements during prayer – all these could help the religious seeker move from thinking about God to being with God, being in God. In each generation certain leaders became acknowledged as religious masters and people flocked to hear them speak or teach.

At the beginning of the twentieth century Martin Buber gathered together many of the stories about these teachers. He published a masterful compilation, *Tales of the Hasidim*, emphasising the down-to-earth approach of early Hasidic practice which tried to bypass arid intellectualism in favour of a direct appeal to the senses. In his chapter on the great Dov Baer of Mezritch (d. 1772) nicknamed 'the *Maggid*'/the preacher, Buber records the story 'of a certain Rabbi Leib, son of Sarah, who once said this: "I did not go to the *Maggid* in order to hear *Torah* from him, but to see how he unlaces his felt shoes and laces them up again." '

Rabbi Leib doesn't want to hear words of moral uplift from Dov Baer. He wants to watch him, not listen to him. But how does a preacher teach through how he ties his shoes? How can this physical, bodily activity be a source of spiritual inspiration? When I first came across this story in my late teens I found it amusing but somewhat arch, a typical piece of religious affectation. Kitsch. I only came to understand it, and appreciate it, some years later when I spent a few months studying in Jerusalem, in a traditional academy of Jewish learning, a *yeshivah*: an Orthodox religious college which specialises in taking Jewish youngsters from secular or non-practising backgrounds and introducing them to traditional religious life.

We had one teacher, Rav Munk, originally from Germany, who had retired to Jerusalem after a long and successful rabbinical career in Golders Green, London. He was very old and very frail, and I remember almost nothing of what he said during the months I took his class. But I do remember how, halfway through the morning, he would give us a short break, and would then proceed very slowly, painstakingly, to take out from his bag a small flask. Carefully, attentively, he would unscrew the top, and with delicate and meticulous movements, like handling a baby, pour some tea into the accompanying cup. He would pause for a few moments, his lips would just quiver with the words of a religious blessing – words heard only by himself and (I'm sure he believed) his Creator – and then with quiet faithfulness he would sip his tea.

I was in awe, spellbound. His mindfulness was an inspiration. Daily, I waited for those few minutes while everyone else went off for a cigarette and I could watch and absorb devotion in action. Through how he drank his tea, Rav Munk taught a form of reverence, of practical spirituality, which had more impact on me than all the traditional knowledge he imparted through his formal words as a teacher. I have always been grateful for this lesson in how paying attention to the physical, bodily details of everyday life can give us an opening to 'infinity in the palm of your hand and eternity in an hour'.

Body and spirit

But of course Jews hardly have a monopoly on teaching spiritual insights through the body. The most important text of yoga philosophy, the Bhagavad Gita, was written around two and a half thousand years ago and lists 18 different types of yoga. Many of these are now available in the West and those who practise regularly report improvements in physical health as well as in a general sense of well-being. Coughs, colds, flu, ear infections, aches and pains seem to diminish in frequency; immune systems can become stronger; circulation and skin tone may improve. The work on posture and breathing releases more energy within the body and allows it both to heal itself and to ward off some of these common complaints.

And then there are all the other opportunities for body-based self-expression. Activities like aerobics, jogging, martial arts, skateboarding, weight-training – a plethora of pursuits which stretch and test and exercise our bodies with all the concentrated rigour and discipline that religious believers once exerted on behalf of their souls, in lives dedicated to penitence, charity and prayer. Of course the emphasis now is different: it is on choice, self-expression, creativity, fitness, health – the body as a source of value in itself.

One could say that all of this body-focused activity is the antithesis of spirituality. It can be self-indulgent and narcissistic. There's even a whiff of the fascistic in aspects of this devotion to the body. But in a secular world, the spiritual can be found in the most unlikely of places, places left open by the decline in religious belief, and the failure in the West for religion to keep itself open to the always elusive but always present spirit of divinity, of Being, which can manifest itself wherever and whenever we are open to it – even in the gym. How presumptuous it can appear if we decide in advance where spirituality can and cannot be present. There is no domain of human activity in which the human spirit cannot reveal itself – and no domain where it will automatically reveal itself.

Bodily aliveness

Freud coined the term *psychoanalyse* to describe his new method of working: 'psychoanalysis' – literally, 'the examination of the soul'. And psychoanalysis gradually developed its own understandings of how the body is one of the clearest windows on to the soul, the psyche, the essential self of each human being. Indeed it has suggested that our conventional Cartesian understanding of our bodies as somehow separate from our 'selves' may be quite misguided.

At the very beginning of life, suggests the British psychoanalyst D. W. Winnicott, our instinctual life as babies is rooted in bodily experiences. When things go well we are

25

'kept warm, handled and bathed and rocked and named'. A sense of 'bodily aliveness' grows out of the bits of experience we garner from both our flesh-and-blood biological being ('soma') and what we imaginatively make of those experiences ('psyche'): 'Human nature is not a matter of mind and body – it is a matter of interrelated psyche and soma, with the mind as a flourish on the edge of psychosomatic functioning.' Mothers help us, through their ongoing care and attention, to gather together the bits of experience so that the developing infant can, from time to time, experience themselves as 'one whole being'. But if things do not go smoothly enough – if this primary sense of 'going-on-being' is ruptured, or too jaggedly disturbed, or too jarringly interrupted – then we, the developing child, are forced to rely (that is over-rely) on our minds to keep ourselves going.

We become good at thinking, rationalising, having a mind of our own. Not so good at feeling connected to, or listening to, or living in, our bodies. In later life bodies can feel too dangerous: they speak to us of our desires and hungers, our need to connect to others, our dependence, our frailty, our mortality. Mental life can be an escape from the rigours and passions of lives incarnated in bodily form. Spirituality and religion are often used as escapes from the body. But our bodies know who we really are. Our bodies have memories, hopes, intelligence. They teach us about ourselves. They are more intimate with our essential selves than our conscious minds allow. They are our spirit in tangible form.

A final, personal vignette. An experience with my own analyst, which occurred several years into my work with him. He usually dressed in a manner I think of as 'smart-casual', often a shirt and jacket, sometimes a tie, occasionally a polo-neck jumper – unexceptional, sober, I suppose quite conventional. But one day I saw that he was wearing a sweater, a green ribbed pullover, which had a huge hole in one sleeve. I can't say this was exactly a transformational moment in the analysis, but it has stayed with me long after all his words have disappeared from consciousness.

Because for me there was something very human about this. It was kind of benign carelessness, or carefreeness, that was somewhat in tension with the contained carefulness with which he phrased his interpretations and observations. That elusive capacity to be at ease with oneself was what I read into this gaping hole. (Other patients would doubtless have read quite different things into it.) For me it signified a kind of relaxedness in relation to himself – which I suppose was what I needed for myself.

Once again, the body illuminated a lesson that language itself could not convey.

Creativity

This is what we are, what we civilize ourselves to disguise – the terrifying human animal in us, the exalted, transcendent, self-destructive, untrammelled lord of creation. We raise each other to the heights of joy. We tear each other limb from fucking limb.

Salman Rushdie, Fury

'Artist's block'

Claire was in her fifties when she first came to see me. She was suffering, she said, from 'artist's block'. She wanted to talk about her painting and why she could no longer find subjects to excite her: why life had become flat, uninteresting. Something was getting in the way of her enthusiasm, her creativity.

Our psychotherapeutic conversations were lively, meandering, mutually stimulating. But I felt Claire was trying hard, perhaps too hard: to be interesting; to 'make progress'; to be a 'good patient'. Something was missing. And then came a session which sparked a memory: 'I remember my parents were entertaining guests – I was four years old – and they wanted me to go to bed, but I was creating, so my daddy picked me up, and I was screaming and kicking, and he took me up to my room and put me over his knee and smacked me for how I'd been downstairs . . .'

Claire was shaking with rage and outrage. The memory was shameful, disturbing – and baffling: why had it emerged now? It felt significant; but what, she wondered, had it got to do with her 'artist's block'? I asked her what she made of her description of what had provoked her father's angry assault: 'I was *creating* . . .' What had she been 'creating'? And why was it such a threat to her parents?

As we talked, we came to see how her 'creativity' had been disregarded, had become bad, had been punished. How her creativity was fused inside her with pain, with anger, and with the suppression of anger. What she had unconsciously, spontaneously, called her 'creating' was her own way of describing both her intense desire to be allowed to interact with the adult world downstairs, and her protest when this natural instinctive self-expressiveness was thwarted and denied. In 'creating' she was expressing her innate wish to show to the world what was inside her (to let the adults see something about herself that would otherwise have to remain hidden) and her fury when this life force was dammed (and damned) up.

Over time, Claire's decades-worth of accumulated furies emerged – and her 'block' gradually dissolved. And as she became less compliant in her relationship to me, she found new energy, new freedom to bring forth out of herself what she wished to communicate to the world, what she wished others to see of herself. She was released into the ordinary mysteries of the creative process. Creativity: the doing that arises out of being.

Artistic creativity and creative living

What is this so-called 'creative process'? Perhaps we should distinguish between artistic creativity and everyday personal creativity. The first may require some special talent – or at least training – though in our egalitarian age we are often told that creativity dwells innately in everyone. Perhaps it does. We all can feel the urge to make something new – with tools, with our hands, with our words – or just to have a new thought (which may remain our secret).

But beneath our creative activities lies something more basic: our capacity to *live* creatively. Our capacity to feel that we are alive, that we are ourselves, that we are not just complying with the world (and those in it) or reacting to it, nor are we dominating the world with our demands on it. But that we exist in the world *which is there for us* as we engage with it, look at it, reach into it. Creative living is rooted in our being in the world in our own unmistakably personal way. We like the feel of silk, and enjoy avocado salad, and want our bathroom painted porcelain blue, and laugh at cartoons, and cry when we see cherry blossoms in first bloom. We are *being* in the world, creating it for ourselves moment by moment.

Yet if this is living creatively, self-expressively, we still know that artistic creativity is something else. Art, literature, religion, philosophy, drama, music, poetry, science, psychotherapy – we constantly create forms to express our questions, give shape to our intuitions, provide structures in our quest for understanding or frameworks to express our knowledge and our desires. The roots of cultural creativity lie in our attempts to make imaginative sense of our own experiences:

> Actors, writers and artists work at the interface between the real and the imagined. They coax us out of the numbness of the everyday – where life passes in a blur – and into the heightened space where we can inhabit other lives and find

ourselves in other circumstances. The mind opens, stretches, takes in more than it knows, and returns again to the ordinary world, richer. This is not just relief – it is revelation.

Jeanette Winterson, novelist

Humankind has struggled for millennia to find ways to express creatively the 'heightened space' where questions of meaning can be explored. Through the poetry of legend, the mystery of myth, the vision of religion, the revelatory efflorescence of art, the dazzling exactitudes of science, we pour out our wish to be like unto God, 'lord of creation'.

'In the beginning . . .'

'In the beginning, God created the heaven and the earth . . .' The great mythic drama of Western consciousness, the Bible, opens with a portrait of a creator: a mysterious force giving purposeful form and imaginative shape to creation. An artist–designer–choreographer shaping and ordering a world which comes into being moment by moment. Does this majestic image offer us a model for human creativity? It depends on how we read it. And that hinges on how we translate the Hebrew text. Every translation is an interpretation.

The influential Biblical commentator, the medieval scholar Rashi, looked at the grammatical form of the first word of this poetic text – *B'reshit* – and saw that it is not free-standing, but introduces a dependent clause: 'In the beginning *of . . .*' Because there are no verse divisions in the original Hebrew text, this suggests that the opening of the Bible should be read at one stretch, as a continuous thought. Something like: '*In the beginning of God's creation of heaven and earth – the earth being unformed and void, with darkness over the deep and an energy from God sweeping over the water – God said: "Let there be light" and there was light.*'

So how did the creation begin? According to this

31

translation–interpretation, the original creative process begins with God 'speaking': 'Let there be . . .' Rashi's reading is thus in agreement with the author of the fourth gospel: 'In the beginning was the word.' Existence is formed out of language. Here the Hebrew Bible distances itself from other contemporary creation themes. There are no divine genealogies or battles between the gods, no rituals to be re-enacted to ensure the supremacy of the national god. All of that is abandoned in favour of the 'word', the *logos* of John's Greek text, the logic of the beginning – a beginning through speech. In this view of creation, time and chronology are subservient to language. 'Time . . . worships language' (W. H. Auden).

So the creative process is an act of articulation by 'God'. Within the Jewish mystical tradition the universe is created out of the 22 letters of the Hebrew alphabet, and their continuing combination and re-combination makes up the substance of our being and that of the world. All of matter, including ourselves (our human 'being'), is but prolongations of this initial Word from the divine 'Being'; echoes, responses, reverberations from the original creative transmission. With the same simple mystery that one of our own thoughts becomes transformed into speech, 'Let there be light' flows into 'and there was light' – in Hebrew the two phrases are identical. One whole, undivided event. The biblical author imagines a beginning in which thought, word and deed are a single creative moment.

This is akin to the popular view of artistic creativity as occurring in a flash of inspiration, as if the whole of what is to be laboured over is given to the aspiring artist in a moment of revelation. Suddenly everything is just there. There are artists' accounts which reinforce this view, but they are in the minority. More frequent are accounts of the creative process which suggest that something very different takes place in the struggle to produce something out of nothing. And this takes us to a second, and radically different, reading of our creation story.

tohu va'vohu

The Authorised Version of the Bible (1613) opens in familiar, imperious fashion:

> 1) In the beginning God created the heaven and the earth. 2) Now the earth was unformed and void, and darkness was upon the face of the deep; and the spirit of God hovered over the face of the waters. 3) And God said: 'Let there be light.' And there was light.

Contrary to initial appearances, this is not a creation out of nothing (*ex nihilo*). The first verse stands as a kind of prologue, a title or headline for the subsequent events: 'The following is the story of how, in the beginning, God created the heavens and the earth.' Full stop. Verse 2 then provides, quite literally, a pro-logue. What existed *before* the logic of God's speaking-the-world-into-being: a primeval void.

What in our first reading was relegated to a subclause as the main narrative moved commandingly on, is here given its full weight. And suddenly we see the huge reservoir of potentially destructive forces that exist before God speaks:

– 'The unformed and void': *tohu va'vohu* (i.e. 'chaos and confusion').

– And 'darkness'.

– And 'the deep' (i.e. 'the chasm, the abyss').

Here we discover – with surprise? with anxiety? – that God does not create everything. For example, the 'darkness' exists independently, before the light. In this reading of the creative process there is drama, struggle, even a sense of improvisation – an essential insecurity about the whole enterprise.

According to one ancient rabbinic homiletic commentary, the world did not spring forth all at once from God's

33

omnipotent will, but 26 attempts preceded the creation. All of which were doomed to failure. The world as we now have it came out of the chaotic midst of this earlier wreckage. Sounds like the stuff of primitive science fiction? Perhaps. But this tradition of the fragility and impermanence of the creative process is spiritually and psychologically significant. For here humanity is an experiment. There is always the risk of failure and the return to chaos and nothingness. The uncertainty of every aspiring artist reverberates within this stream of mythic thinking. God's anxious cry of hope – 'If only this time it will last!' – accompanies human history, and our own lives within it.

Our first reading invited us into a harmonious world of language, logic and ordered inevitability. Our second reading opens up the possibility that insecurity and impermanence is inbuilt within the fabric of our consciousness and creativity. A world where things fall into place, and make sense; where there is order and security. And a world of 'chaos and confusion' accompanying the unfolding of everyday life.

Our lives stretch out between the two. We balance on a very narrow bridge. How do we avoid the abyss? Momentarily our attention is drawn to something else, creatively alive within us. A kind of inner knowing. Within the darkness, our own idiosyncratic 'Let there be light . . .' A spark of eternity illuminating us, echoing within us, from the Source.

Dreams

When I write a story, I try to go to sleep with one
unfinished idea, an idea I haven't got to the bottom
of. The hope is that at night, in my dreams, it will
ripen.

David Grossman, Israeli novelist

Buried treasure

A story is told about a poor man, Eizik son of Yekel, of
Krakow. One night he had a dream. He was in Prague
standing next to the bridge which leads to the king's palace.
And he heard a voice saying: 'A treasure is buried under
here.' He dismissed the dream. He had problems enough;
and anyway the journey would be long, and exhausting. But
the dream returned, and when it recurred a third time Eizik
prepared for the journey and set out for Prague.

After several days he reached the city and found the
bridge; but it was guarded day and night and he did not
dare to start digging. Day after day he went to the bridge
and waited indecisively until evening. Finally the captain of
the guards, who had been watching him hovering around,
accused him of being a spy. Too frightened to invent a story,

Eizik told the truth: a dream of buried treasure had brought him here from a distant land.

The captain smiled: 'You're such a fool, paying attention to a dream and wearing yourself out like this! Listen: if I'd had faith in dreams, I would have travelled to Krakow long ago. For I used to dream of a treasure buried there under the bed of a Jew . . . Eizik, son of Yekel, that was his name. But can you imagine going from house to house searching for the right man and an imaginary dream treasure?' Eizik thanked him, travelled home and dug under his bed – where he found the treasure.

This is an old story. Variations are found in the folk literature of many cultures. An individual makes a journey, following a dream, a vision, an intuition. They are looking for a treasure; and a journey is necessary; and there are hardships on the way; and something unexpected is discovered; and the traveller returns; and all is the same. And everything is different.

Finding the treasure

How literally do we take our dreams? In the original version of this story, as told by the Hasidic master Nachman of Bratslav (1772–1810), he adds the following moral: 'Now you know that the treasure is always with you – but to find out about it you have to journey far away: to a *zaddik* [a spiritual guide]'. But when Martin Buber retells this same parable he concludes with the comment: 'There is something you cannot find anywhere in the world, not even at the *zaddik*'s . . . It is a great treasure, which may be called the fulfillment of existence. The place where this treasure can be found is the place on which one stands.'

Whereas Nachman of Bratslav stresses the importance of a literal understanding of the role of the dream in the story – listen to the dream, make a journey, find a teacher who will point you in the right direction – in Buber's existentialist reading of the story, spiritual guides and gurus and other 'experts' cannot help individuals find the meaning and fulfilment of their lives. There is no external authority. Truth is to be found within each person. The dream in the story, Buber suggests, has to be *interpreted symbolically* rather than acted out.

In Buber's understanding of the story, the 'treasure' we each possess is to be claimed in everyday life, in whatever situation we happen to find ourselves: 'The environment which I feel to be the natural one, the situation which has been assigned to me as my fate, the things that happen to me day after day, the things that claim me day after day – these contain my essential task and such fulfillment of existence as is open to me.' We find our 'Self' where we find ourselves. 'Paradise' can be experienced wherever we happen to be.

Thankfully, there is no 'correct' reading of this story. Like the best of our dreams it is open to more than one interpretation. On one level it is beautifully simple. To find the treasure Eizik has to move away from the familiar and explore the world. He arrives back where he started and knows the place for the first time. He finds what was available to him all along but which he'd never realised was there for him, and him alone.

On another level the story is beautifully ambiguous. Eizik has to make the journey to find out that the journey wasn't necessary. But, paradoxically, the journey was necessary otherwise he wouldn't have found out what he needed to know. Like an Escher print, we can locate ourselves within the story – which is the story of our lives – but cannot catch hold of how the whole picture holds together. For a moment we think we glimpse the secret. We feel we discover an unequivocal place from which to see how our lives work, or what we might need to do to make them work. But then what we know (or think we know) is gone, as fleeting as a dream.

37

Psychotherapy and dreams: the cinema of the self

How can we learn to understand our dreams? Or if not to understand them, then at least to give them space to intrigue us, provoke us, inspire us? For as the contemporary British psychoanalyst Adam Phillips puts it: 'Whether or not dreams are meaningful, they are good to make meaning with.' As a psychotherapist and a rabbi I feel that I am an heir to two traditions which have always taken seriously both dreams and dreamers.

As a psychotherapist I stand within a chain of tradition that stretches back to Freud, who called dreams 'the royal road to the unconscious'. By which he meant that dreams can provide us with a significant way into our hidden selves: those layers of experience and memory, hopes and wishes, which are part of who we are but might be too distressing or too exciting to hold consciously in mind. Through the technique he called 'free association' – saying whatever came to mind without censoring the thoughts – he encouraged his patients to allow themselves to make use of a dream's images. Together with the analyst they could burrow deeply into parts of themselves that they had had cause to repress or hide away out of fear or shame or pain.

Although Freud's seminal work, *The Interpretation of Dreams*, was an almost complete failure when it was published in 1900 – it sold just 351 copies in its first six years – it came to be seen as one of the intellectual cornerstones of the twentieth century. But from the very beginning of psychoanalysis there were those who disagreed with Freud's understanding of how the mind worked. This was true even among his colleagues, let alone a wider public scandalised by his insistence that a sexual substratum underlies all human activity and thinking.

His Swiss colleague C. G. Jung developed a different approach to dreams from that of his Viennese mentor. Freud believed that a dream's images *disguised* parts of the dreamer's life that she or he might not want to know about consciously – and so one had to follow the dreamer's associations (and resistances to associations) to zigzag into the deeper meanings hidden in the dream's symbols. Jung believed that the dream picture contained all the material necessary to understand the message the dream was trying to convey. Through *amplification* of the dream's images and a process he called 'active imagination', Jung felt that a person's psyche (the whole of our being, conscious and unconscious) could be relied upon to direct the seeker towards his or her goal – the expression of the 'Self'. A dream's images might remind the dreamer or the analyst of myths, fairytales, or other cultural expressions – and contact with these collective ideas would help to heal the dreamer. Because, Jung believed, they were part of a larger numinous dimension of existence, the world of the sacred: 'the gods'.

Although these are two very different approaches towards finding meaning within dreams, what they share – a belief in and respect for the integrity and inherent meaningfulness of dreams – is more important than their differences. And this belief seems to be a universal cultural phenomenon: since earliest history dreams have been regarded as holding significance either for the individual or for the dreamer's wider social or national group. They were spiritual resources, giving access to a dimension of being hidden from one's everyday gaze.

In our own era, no area of the social sciences or artistic culture was unaffected by Freud's speculations on the unconscious. And the cinema above all, the twentieth century's new art-form, became a veritable theatre of dreams. The Spanish director Luis Buñuel thought of the cinema as a form of human expression resembling the work of the mind during sleep: 'Film seems to be an involuntary imitation of sleep. The darkness that invades the auditorium is the equivalent of closing our eyes.' Sitting in the dark, mesmerised, cinema audiences were induced into collective dreaming. And the influence of this cultural form of group dreaming flows the other way too. In our individual dreams we now borrow the conventions (montage, jump-cuts, slow-motion etc.) as well as the characters, themes and imagery of the films we see.

'Interpretations belong to God'

Of course Freud himself was part of another chain of tradition, one which had always acknowledged the spiritual value of dreams. The chain starts with that extraordinary dream of the Jewish people that we call the Hebrew Bible: the record – visioned and documented with as much awareness as was possible – of one people's encounter with the transcendent. A great bringing-to-our-attention of collective experience. A recounting of half-forgotten, reworked and remembered holy moments, that nevertheless feels as if it's been recorded almost unconsciously.

The Bible is the 'dream work' of the Jewish people: what is left over after the supposed events have dissolved into the collective consciousness of the people. An amalgam of wishes, fears, desires, images, stories containing all the anxieties and hopefulness of a people generating meaning for themselves from within the flux and chaos of historical time. And biblical sentences (like dreams) contain compressed and condensed meanings which call out for that special kind of attention we call interpretation.

In an Egyptian dungeon Pharaoh's anxious and un-comprehending butler comes with a dream to a Hebrew fellow-prisoner. And what does Joseph, the Bible's great dreamer, say to him? 'Do not interpretations belong to God? So, please tell me . . .' (Genesis 40:8). Let's tease out the ambiguities here.

Joseph's words are enigmatic. Literally they mean 'Are not interpretations from *Elohim* = God = "the gods" = the transcendent realm'. This confounds our expectations. It is not the *dreams themselves* that come from somewhere else, but their *interpretations*. The text doesn't question where the dreams come from: they are ours. But, says Joseph, the meanings we make from them – or how we use them to make meaning – comes from another place of understanding: the divine. But this seems to be the divine ('the gods') in us, in another part of our consciousness. Which is why he continues: 'So, please, tell *me* . . .' Through a conversation between them, meaning will come into being.

Our dreams present us with messages from unknown parts of ourselves. But only we have the answers to the questions they pose. What journeys do we need to make – to where? to whom? – before we return home to our beds and discover the treasures that lie within our own ripening stories?

Emotions

It is difficult to discuss feelings when the TV speaks so loudly; cries so operatically; seems always, in everything, one step ahead. Yet people continue to manage this awesome trick of wrestling sentiment away from TV's colonisation of all things soulful and human . . .

Zadie Smith, novelist

'How are you?'

You bump into a friend on the street, or at a party. 'How are you?' they ask, in that polite sociable way we all affect. I usually find myself overcome with a momentary panic. 'How *am* I?', I wonder (I can be quite a literalist sometimes). And usually I don't know. Or I know that I'm feeling many different things but at that moment can't catch hold of any of them. So I find myself responding, hesitantly, that 'I'm fine' – this is simpler than saying 'Don't ask me that, it's much too difficult a question'. Or I say 'Not so bad' – that traditional British emotional disclaimer meaning 'Not so good – but I don't want to talk about it'. Whatever I stumble towards as an answer, I know that I dread the question. And I don't think I'm alone.

'How we feel' presents us with a dilemma. How honest can we be? With the questioner – or with ourselves? Because underneath the outer performance of our selves, the performance that we feel we need in order to get by in the world, something else is going on. Something to do with the fraught realities of our human condition. Our minds, our bodies, our emotions – and the overlapping connections between them – all cause us fretful days and sleepless nights.

Mind, body, emotions

Our minds may be active but they can also make us forgetful, uncertain, indecisive. We lie awake at night, worrying away at our problems. We're 'all over the place' we say, or we're 'falling to pieces'. We may feel we're disintegrating, or spiralling down into a black hole from which there is no way out, no way back. There's so much talk these days about stress – but the origin of the word stress is distress. No talk of our states of mind is possible without it leading us on to our emotions.

And what of our bodies – that site of both pleasure and regret? Let's leave aside (for now) sex with all its vicissitudes: its needs, its fears, its desires and where they take us. Our bodies themselves cause us anxiety: how young they look, how fit or fat, how soft or smooth or scarred. And our bodies give us pain. We try to protect them and look after them, but they are exposed to the ravages of time and decay. We age, our bodies stop working as they once did, they stop working as we wish them to. One day they will give up altogether. One day we will die. We can't talk about our bodies without it leading straight to our feelings.

So what about our emotions? If we spoke of them truly, fully, faithfully what would we say? At our best, we know the diverse richness of our emotional states. We can be generous and nurturing, compassionate and strong, capable of honesty and courageousness, selflessness and love and sacrifice. We can feel happy. We can feel that life is worthwhile. And we can laugh – we have a sense of humour.

But we are not always at our best. Although this sumptuousness of feeling is a part of the story for all of us, it is not the whole story, for any of us. For there is also heartbreak, beneath the surface. There is suffering, upset, sorrow, grief. There is loneliness. There is also jealousy, greed and envy. There is anger, bitterness and vengeful destructive feelings. There are self-destructive feelings. We cause hurt and suffer hurt. Personal relationships disappoint us. Family relationships break down. Loving relationships end. And people we love die. There is helplessness, that becomes hopelessness. There is futility, and despair. When are we allowed on our journey through life to say that we are hurting? When can we stop pretending? When can we say that we are vulnerable and fragile and frightened people?

What can 'spirituality' say about these facts of life? How can we develop a spiritual perspective that does not deny emotional pain? Is it possible to develop a way of *being with* our selves – our minds and bodies and feelings – that does not abandon the integrity of what we feel but at the same time does not allow our emotions to dictate our lives?

For we are not only our minds. We are not only our bodies. We are not only our emotions. What makes each of us unique is our human spirit, our soul. Perhaps it is the loss of our sense of soul that is our greatest distress of all. For beneath the heartache is the 'soul-ache'.

Soul-ache

One of my favourite prayers comes at the beginning of the Jewish morning service:

> My God, the soul you have given me is pure. You created it,

44

you formed it, you made it live within me. You watch over
it within me, but one day you will take it from me . . .

The rhythm of the prayer reverberates inside me. I roll it
over, on my tongue, in my mind. What a thought, this
fragment of ancient wisdom, this reminder from the depths
of a tradition that we too have depths. That a mystery surrounds our life. That in spite of all the problems we
experience through having a mind and a body and
emotions, there is something else too, animating us, 'being'
in us, being us. Something that is 'pure': that is undisturbed
by, uncorrupted by, unconstrained by the dominance of our
emotions in our day-to-day lives.

But our souls get battered and bruised. All that emotional
turbulence that buffets them. All that swirling around of our
thoughts and feelings and bodily needs and sensations. The
poor soul, our essential self, cowers in the face of the
onslaught. Can we give the soul time and space to 'live
within us'? Can our soul survive in a world that constantly
stirs up our emotions, and tells us that feelings are everything? If our souls are to be enabled to live within us
uncolonised by our emotions, to what realities of feeling do
we need to give attention?

Within the human psyche a Promethean battle rages
between our experiences of love and hate, hope and despair,
contentment and desperation, fullness and emptiness,
comfort and distress, nurture and abandonment. These basic
polarities of our instinctual life form our psychological
makeup from the earliest moments of our existence. The
conflicts between these opposing states-of-mind-and-being
become part of the fabric of our experience of being alive in
the world, the warp and weft of everyday life. From birth
onwards the unceasing struggle between our creative and
destructive impulses shadows our lives.

The unformed chaotic state of being described at the very
beginning of Genesis – *tohu va'vohu* – is a metaphor for these

45

aspects of early infantile experience. From infancy onwards we form defences to keep out the forces of chaos within us, sea-walls to resist the waves of feeling that flood our developing psyches. As we develop, and through the process of socialisation and education, we find ways of containing or transforming these elemental energies within ourselves. Within the biblical myth, God fills the formless space with creative activity, just as we have to fill our lives with acts of creativity (and love?) to generate meaning in the face of the void.

But this work is bruising and exhausting. And for many it is confusing, beyond belief. We are, from our earliest moments onwards, dependent, symbol-forming, myth-making creatures, seeking security, containment and human contact in the face of powerful inner experiences of need-iness and helplessness. Religion, traditionally, has attempted to address these needs and feelings, yet has invariably done so without understanding their origins within an indi-vidual's early psychological development, nor the unconscious power such feelings exert within adult life.

Western religions attempt to create a safe haven, a frame-work of thought and action within which the believer can find sustenance and guidance and security, while the battle between our creative and destructive capacities, between 'good' and 'evil', is being waged. Thus the obvious attraction of religious systems, institutions and leaders offering clear answers to the confusions and passions of life. The capacity to tolerate uncertainty and ambivalence – the hallmark of mature psychological and spiritual health – is in distinct tension with religious standpoints which offer unqualified definitions of what is true and what is false, of what is good practice and what is bad faith.

Only if due space and attention is given to the mental and physical and emotional dimensions to our lives, in all their grandeur and misery, can there then be room for our souls too to breathe, to glow. Like the artist who has to prepare her canvas before the painting can emerge, like the novelist who keeps a work-journal before his fiction can come forth, like the pianist who spends hours on scales and fingering before a performance, we need to prepare the ground for our souls. Paying attention to our emotional development can pave the way for our spiritual selves to emerge from the quagmire of feelings in which we are daily immersed.

Our emotional dramas

Over the last few years we have been living through a quiet revolution in Britain. The stiff upper lip is being replaced by the quivering lip. This is a revolution born of the need for intimacy. In the past devotion to a religion could help people feel close: to one another; to a culture of values and meaning; to their God. But what happens to our need for such intimacy when our devotional aid is the TV set?

The reaction to the death of Princess Diana symbolised this sea-change in our society. People came on to the streets with shrines of flowers, with prayers, with that spiritual impulse for reflection and active devotion because they felt, accurately or not, that they had lost someone who cared, and someone with whom they felt they had an intimate connection.

Some of Diana's favourite images of herself were those where she was captured tearfully, Madonna-like, holding a sick or injured child. In that extraordinary combination of selflessness and self-regard she presented herself to us as caring, loving, compassionate, healing. She was the fantasy of our potential, how we would like to think of ourselves, how we would like to be. But simultaneously she was also a reflection of our everyday, fallible selves: marital troubles, doubts about her looks, an eating disorder, vengeful, having therapy, perpetually searching for happiness. And all her flaws becoming virtues by dint of that compulsive, self-revelatory style which now passes for honesty in a culture, conditioned by daytime confessional TV, where emotion equals honesty, and tears mean sincerity.

But during this transformation in our society, how alert are we to this confusion between show and substance? How do we learn to discriminate between true and false emotion, between image and reality? Jewish historical experience recalls the terrifying consequences of living in societies dominated by group emotions unchecked by the counter-balance of reason, rationality, analytical intelligence. Developing one's own emotional literacy is quite different from the emotional bulimia which disgorges undigested feelings into the public domain.

The average Briton now watches 3 hours and 41 minutes of TV a night. In a culture increasingly dominated by manu-factured images and soap opera-style feelings, can the soul survive the drama of our emotions? Can we develop a spiri-tuality, both robust and sensitive, which can help us attune to that unseen Presence that lies beyond the image and behind the feelings?

Food

> In the cupboards [of the Jewish home] holy and
> secular meet and jostle, there is no strain, for all
> things can be transformed if they are turned to God.
> Cocktail cabinets and the kitchen drawer are the
> sacristy for the liturgy of the home.
>
> *Rabbi Lionel Blue*

A taste of heaven

My first religious retreat – I was a young rabbinical student –
was led by Lionel Blue. We met in a windy, ramshackle
retreat centre in Sussex. With a dozen of my colleagues we
practised sitting in silence – always so hard for Jews to do.
We practised our newly acquired theological debating
skills – so cerebral and divorced from reality as we tried to
impress our peers. We practised our snooker – no problems
there. And we practised our cooking – the retreat was self-
catering, such a shock for young Jewish men in the 1970s.

I remember the frustrations of this new discipline called
silence – so alien, so 'Christian' to my provincial Jewish
mind. Yet I also remember the frustrations of talking, of
discussions which so easily turned to arguments. Surely this

wasn't the way to experience the spiritual? But above all I remember the food. And in particular the cauliflower soup served up to us by Lionel on a cold November evening. He had disappeared from our afternoon's wrangling, and with an economy of effort and more than a soupçon of un-rehearsed love, produced food which spoke more eloquently of the spirit than all our high-flown Talmudic portentous-ness. This was food for – and from – the soul. It tasted, so to speak, of heaven.

For Lionel, the preparing and cooking and eating and sharing of food was a primary medium for spiritual self-expressiveness. And the cupboards and cabinets and drawers of the Jewish home contained the artefacts of Jewish spiritu-ality: the candlesticks and breadcovers and winecups for the Sabbath, lying neglected during the week, but capable of transforming secular time into holy living when the hour was right. Indeed any gathering of convivial souls, where food was honoured, was a form of secular transubstan-tiation: God made present through the bonds of family, friends, guests, brought together to celebrate the joys of sharing food, hospitality and intimacy.

He reminded us that the celebrant at the Passover meal in the home begins the annual ceremony with the words: 'Let all who are hungry, come and eat!' The invitation is to assuage one's hunger (literally and metaphorically) on the ritual psychodrama about to unfold, with its symbol-laden foods and lesson in collective history. The Passover cele-bratory meal calls us back to our own childhood and the childhood of the Jewish people. 'Theologies alter and beliefs may die, but smells always remain in memory.'

Lionel taught me how – like the Mass or the Eucharist ceremony, the Hindu food offering to the gods, the Sikh *kara prashad* holy sweet, the Muslim *shir kurma* dessert at the end of Ramadan, and the Buddhists in Japan celebrating with red beans and rice – Jewish food too can have spiritual provenance. And that the spiritual and the material realms are, for those who have eyes to see, noses to smell and taste-buds to savour it, two aspects of one reality.

One hundred blessings

But how do we learn to experience the material and the spiritual as one? Or rather, how can we learn that the material world in which we are immersed is suffused with opportunities for experiencing that enhanced sense of being we call the spiritual? In our first chapter I suggested that our capacity for awe and wonder depends upon our attentive-ness to what is happening in us and around us moment by moment. And I want to return to that theme now in relation to food – both in its literal sense, and in its metaphorical sense of the experiences we take into ourselves that nurture us, our humanity and our sensitivity to the unfolding mystery that is life.

One of the ideas within my own Jewish tradition that has always delighted (and daunted) me is the principle that we are to find occasions to offer a hundred blessings a day. A 'blessing' in this context is a combination of things. It is an opportunity to pause from our immersion in the flood of daily events. An opportunity for thankfulness. An oppor-tunity for acknowledging our dependence on the huge chain of being in which we are just one tiny (but infinitely significant) link. An opportunity to take our noses from the grindstone, the harshness of life, and experience an inner freedom, a freedom of the spirit.

Judaism offers those who live within its embrace many structured opportunities for this form of attentiveness. Often these opportunities become duty, or heavy with over-familiarity. They may be performed mindlessly rather than mindfully. But you certainly don't have to be Jewish – indeed it may be easier if you are not – to appreciate their inner purpose. A range of formalised blessings dispersed through the day and the working week can heighten our sensitivity towards the spiritual dimension of being. Yet the goal of finding a hundred opportunities a day to experience the wonder of being seems impossibly demanding.

Jewish tradition recognised this and, ever pragmatic, cheats a little. If you are devout, reciting the set prayers which are prescribed for the faithful three times a day, then most of these hundred blessings are incorporated like formulae into the prayer services. So you've fulfilled your responsibility almost without thinking about it. Which sort of defeats the original intention. For the ancient rabbinic principle of the hundred blessings was designed to provide 'food' for the soul, something to set against the incessant demands of the material world, the world in which we lose our vision, our higher aspirations, our place in the scheme of things – fragile and vulnerable, yet of ultimate worth.

Can we find, perhaps not a hundred, but even half a dozen times during the day (or even *once* – because, after all, who's counting?) when we can experience a sense of gratitude or wonder at what life brings us? This challenge can be taken up by anyone, inside or outside a religious tradition. You will want to find your own opportunities, which occur naturally in the course of your day. This cannot be predicted or dictated from the outside. But there are some clues around as to the areas of life where such opportunities can occur.

For example: Judaism has a series of set blessings (though you can make up your own) which surround that most basic and functional activity – eating. So before a meal there is a moment to reflect on our dependence on the natural world which generates our food, as well as the human labour of others which has enabled us to be eating now. There are separate blessings for bread, for cakes and pastries and sweets, for fruit, for vegetables, for wine. As well as a general blessing for all other foods: 'You are blessed, Eternal our God, the energy within existence, through whose word everything has its being.'

Reminders

These blessings are just reminders: they guard against our innate omnipotence, the feeling that we are the centre of the world and that life owes us something. Blessings around food gently remind us that we are fragile, dependent human beings who cannot create our own sustenance. In an age of supermarkets when you can buy anything you want from anywhere in the world regardless of the season, in an era (at least in the West) where hunger is not a problem for the majority of citizens – and indeed overeating has become a major anxiety for so many – such reminders might seem absurdly inconsequential, an irrelevance. And yet in our hearts we know how fortunate (blessed?) we are to have food to eat whenever we want it. A few silently spoken words or thoughts, before eating, keep us sensitive to our good fortune, which we may have done nothing to deserve.

Jewish tradition also maps out a whole variety of other occasions when a blessing can be offered, moments when our consciousness can be heightened. Some seem obvious, others a surprise. There are blessings on seeing the sea, first blossoms, a rainbow, on seeing any wonder of nature. On hearing thunder. On smelling flowers, or smelling spices, or perfumes. On tasting something new. On seeing something beautiful. Our five senses help us transmute mundanity into enhanced awareness.

Then there are various blessings regarding people you might meet: people with religious or secular knowledge and wisdom; royalty; people with disabilities ('You are blessed, Eternal our God, the energy within existence, who varies the forms of creation'). And there are blessings for events like moving into a new home, wearing new clothes, hearing good news, hearing bad news, recovering from an illness, meeting someone who's recovered from illness, on hearing of a death, on seeing a place where something wonderful has happened to you in the past. So many opportunities, day by day, for our radical amazement at the richness of life here on this grain of sand in the cosmos. Our grain of sand.

All these blessings within the Jewish tradition have their own formalised words, but that is just for convenience. Sometimes it's easier to borrow other people's words than find our own. And sometimes silence will be our most devout response. We may or may not believe in a divine energy, a God, 'through whose word everything has its being' or 'who varies the forms of creation', but we know the difference between our souls feeling crushed or oppressed, and when they feel fed. Life presents itself to us and we respond to it: we nurture ourselves through the alchemy of that process. We are co-creators of the worlds we inhabit.

Heaven and hell

Lionel told us a story, during the retreat, about a rabbi who wanted to see both heaven and hell. He fell asleep and dreamt that he was standing before a door, that opened into a room; and the room was prepared for a feast. A table was set and at its centre lay a great dish of delicious hot food. Guests sat around the table with long spoons in their hands, but they were crying out with hunger: the spoons were so long that, however they distorted themselves, they could not get the food into their mouths. Unable to nourish themselves, they cursed God the author of their plight. And the rabbi awoke, knowing he had seen hell.

But he fell asleep again and dreamt that he was standing before a door, that opened into a room; and the room was prepared for a feast. A table was set and at its centre lay a great dish of delicious hot food. Nothing had changed and he was about to cry out in horror. Then he saw that the guests had smiles on their faces, for with the same long spoons they were reaching out across the table to feed each other. And they were giving thanks to God the author of their joy. The rabbi awoke and he too blessed God who had shown him the nature of heaven and hell. And the chasm – a hair's-breadth wide – that divides them.

God

Some of those on the highest floors lived, some of them died. Some of the firemen who went up the stairs lived. Some of them died. All those on the west side when the towers collapsed died. All those on the east side lived. You have to believe God has a plan.

Rudy Giuliani, former mayor of New York City

Belief

I don't believe in Mayor Giuliani's God – the one who is the architect of what happens to us, the creator of our heaven and our hell. I would not have written this book if I did. Sometimes I think that life would be much simpler (though still mysterious) if I had that kind of belief. It is, after all, a traditional form of monotheistic faith. Upheld through the generations by countless men and women who lived their lives – and sometimes gave their lives – holding fast to their belief in a benign deity whose ways, though beyond human understanding, were by definition imbued with justice, righteousness and love, such a faith generates in me contradictory feelings.

On the one hand there is awe at the capacity to transcend doubt and submit to the accumulated wisdom, the inherited discernment, of one's faith tradition; admiration for those who feel so moved by the image of a creating or revealing or redeeming God that they are prepared to mould their lives into behavioural patterns predetermined by a source of authority not their own. But on the other hand, uncomfortably and problematically, I'm also aware of my thinly-disguised irritation with the naïvety, the illogicality, the lack of discriminating thoughtfulness within such uncomplicated piety.

Thus the devotee and the rationalist do battle within me. The secret believer who believes (or wishes to believe) in spite of himself. And the pragmatic doubter who knows that our need to feel looked after by a loving, parental force is a deep and determining human drive – and that our capacity for self-delusion is endless.

Yet when life appears fraught, harsh, bordering on the meaningless – as it does to all of us on occasion, and to some for long swathes of time – what are we aching souls to do? What is there to sustain us, nurture us, console us? What are we to believe in? This book tries to point towards a different kind of belief from that of the old-style theological nostrums of monotheistic faith. A belief wrestled from the discomforting vicissitudes of everyday life, in 'a spirit of respect for the struggling, battered thing which any human soul is' (D. H. Lawrence). A belief which tries to reflect truthfully on our human condition rather than enunciate truths about it. A belief that is not a form of cruelty: a repressive domination of the self in the name of an external authority we call 'God' or 'Tradition'.

Creating meaning

So, what might we want a God for? As human vulnerabilities, fears and needs are so pervasive, humanity has often sought and created a God to meet these needs or to allay these primal fears. Sensations of helplessness, powerlessness and neediness are present in all of us. But we often deny this, and early on in life find (unconscious) ways of defending ourselves from such threatening feelings.

Later, we may find ourselves drawn to a paternal God whom we can look up to and feel loved and protected by. Or a maternal God (even though we might call it 'He') who can hold and nourish us. Or perhaps a potent God (or Goddess) with whose power we can either identify, or in whose immanent presence we can surrender ourself. How deeply we need to feel secure, protected, contained, understood, accepted, loved! And how we search for a 'God' to meet these primary needs. We are attracted to God-images which console and comfort us in the face of a human neediness and fearfulness rooted in our formative years but still alive within us.

But what kind of belief is credible? My bookshelves are bursting with theology books: bravura attempts to provide systematic, objective descriptions of 'divine' reality. As if there could be a 'science' of God. These theologies are vast meaning-generating systems designed to cajole us into viewing life as having an inherent meaning and purpose. They are products of our human need to create order out of chaos, meaning out of randomness.

Monotheism puts its faith in the existence of a Creator of order, a Bestower of meaning: 'God'. Such theologies (just like secular psychoanalytic theories) suggest that everything we do and everything that happens to us is part of a larger picture, of which we can know only a part. Whether they insist that meaning lies in God's hands or within the unconscious, these supposedly authoritative intellectual enterprises help us defend ourselves against the terrifying alternative: meaninglessness.

For millennia, religious systems and teachers struggled to explain to us God's mysterious ways, as if God's ways were facts that existed separately from ourselves. But Immanuel Kant's philosophical enquiry into how the human mind converts formless experience into ordered knowledge led him to a change of viewpoint as revolutionary as that of Copernicus. Kant (1724–1804) saw that the mind does not *receive* and absorb the world in an objective way. We *confer* objectivity on what we experience. The principles by which we make sense of the world are not in a world above us, as Plato had suggested, but in our own heads. Order, moral values and laws are not transcendent. They aren't 'facts' located in a supernatural world, but 'tucked away unnoticed on the near side of experience' (Don Cupitt).

When we realise that the One who creates order out of chaos is us, this spells the end of the objective God of realist theology. When we realise that certain traditional religious images of God are the mythic projections of the human mind, we enter a new and potentially liberating world of thinking. When we speak of God as good or loving or just or suffering or 'having a plan', we are projecting human attributes and qualities on to the 'divine'. We are creating God in our own image.

Existential faith

In the book of Genesis humanity conceived of a conceiver: we gave birth to the idea of something giving birth to the idea of us. It is a wondrous, inspired, inspiring idea. But its anthropomorphism – the personification of God using emotions familiar from our own human experience – makes us think of God as a personality, whose actions are objectively 'true' and 'real'; or whose lack of action then needs to be explained, or explained away.

Yet the remarkable thing about the Biblical narrative is that although it uses a multitude of metaphors, names and images to describe the character it calls 'God', it also draws attention to the limitations (fraudulence?) of this way of thinking about the numinous. At the beginning of the book of Exodus, Moses wants to tell the Israelites that he has had an encounter with the divine. So he asks the power whom he is addressing (and who he conceives of as addressing him) for its 'name'. But the narrative's response from 'God' is enigmatic: 'I am that I am . . . This is what you say to the children of Israel: " 'I am and will be' has sent me to you" ' (3:13–14).

'I am and will be'. What kind of name is that? What the Biblical storytellers are pointing to here is that a fixed, pre-designated name cannot describe 'being', 'is-ness'. An unfolding process cannot be reduced to a static noun. In spite of our human desire to contain and control the un-predictable fluidity of 'that which is and will be' within the safe confines of defined names and labels, an energy which animates the universe (and ourselves within it) cannot be limited in this way. Such an energy is also, unset-tlingly, beyond good and evil.

By the middle of the nineteenth century, the Christian philosopher–theologian Søren Kierkegaard acknowledged that the days of traditional theology were over. He opted instead for a radical re-statement of the religious position. He accepts anthropocentricism: human beings at the centre of spiritual life, using religious ideas not as external con-straints on behaviour but as tools to inspire us and guide us inwardly. He is the father of modern grown-up religious thinking. If there is to be faith in 'God' then it must be subjective and existential.

Kierkegaard's last words were: 'The bomb explodes, and the conflagration will follow.' If God is not 'out there' any more, if God is not 'factual' but a self-constructed ideal which can give worth to our lives, much traditional theo-logical speculation becomes redundant. The old nagging questions – 'Why does God allow this? Does God listen to our prayers or not? How can a good God allow evil?'– become irrelevant to one's spiritual journey.

60

The death of old notions of an external God takes us into uncharted spiritual territory. New questions arise:

– Can we allow a mature spirituality to evolve in us which is not merely an unconscious attempt to solve an emotional problem or satisfy a hidden need?

– If we take back our projections on to 'God', can we recognise our personal dependence and collective inter-dependence on our own human capacities for love, goodness, justice, mercy – all the traditional attributes we ascribed to God?

– To what extent can we acknowledge that *these capabilities are in us*, and their potential is, so to speak, 'divine', limited only by our own personal limitations? (For like the God/s of old we too can be angry, jealous, destructive).

– And have we sufficient humility, self-irony, and sense of humour to put ourselves at the centre without becoming as omnipotent as the God we once had?

Shema

The key seems to be attentiveness. Embedded at the heart of Judaism is a Biblical sentence which has entered the daily liturgy: 'Hear, Israel: the Eternal (*Adonai*) is our God, that which is Eternal is One' (Deuteronomy 6:4). 'Hear' does not do justice to the Hebrew word *shema*. Essentially it means 'pay attention'. The expectation is that, individually and collectively, we have the capacity to develop our attentive-ness. 'Israel' literally means 'the one who struggles with/ against God'. The Bible addresses all who wrestle with God, all who struggle to understand the nature of the divine, the numinous, the mystery of being. The text challenges us to learn to pay active attention to *Adonai*: 'being', 'that which is', 'the Eternal'. In other words: to what is going on moment by moment in us, to us, between us. This is where 'God' is.

The quality of attentiveness we give to ourselves and give to each other is how 'God' is made present, how 'God' is brought into the world. Conventional theology projects this attentiveness on to God and asks that we be the recipients of it. Monotheistic prayers are freighted with requests for God to 'hear' our prayers, our voices, the silent cry of the soul, hear what we cannot say. But it is our own capacity for attentive hearing – an attunement to life we can develop within ourselves – that enables the prayers of others to be responded to, the voices and cries of others to be heard, the wordless needs of others to be attended to. We are dependent on each other. And the quality of our interactions with the world in which we live – with family, friends and strangers – depends on our capacity to *shema*, pay active attention.

If theology is the science of God, then spirituality is the art of God. Creatively alive and evolving God images can perform a vital and healing function for human growth. They can help us describe the moral and spiritual goals of our lives, and help us tolerate suffering and the inevitability of death. But such images, constructed out of our own discriminating intelligence and emotional perceptiveness, might always remain partial and fragmentary, providing us with moments of insight, glimpses of meaning; yet spiralling away from certainties towards a Cubist-like collage where several perspectives are present at the same time.

To come to appreciate that the divine is not 'out there' but in us is the work of a lifetime. And to know that the divine may not just be in us but may also be a reflection of an energy greater than ourselves – that may be revealed in a moment. We proceed by way of paradox. The process of God-making is dialectical. Our 'God' may become both the source of illumination as well as the light towards which we hesitantly move. And the shadows thus formed on our path are One with the unseen light which guides us.

Humour

A person deserves paradise who can make his companions laugh.

The Koran

How do you make God laugh? Tell him your plans.

Yiddish proverb

Laughing well

We live as if we are in control of our lives. We plan our days, our years, as if our fate was (more or less) in our own hands. But when our omnipotence runs up against reality, and we find that things are less in our control than we would wish them to be, what then? Do we rage with frustration – 'It's not fair!' – and shout at our loved ones (a tantrum)? Do we pretend it hasn't happened – 'It wasn't important anyway' – and carry on regardless (a denial)? Do we dissolve in tears, feeling sad and secretly angry (a depression)? Do we become bitter or self-mocking, turning our anger against ourselves: 'I didn't deserve having it, I'm stupid for wanting it in the first place, I should have known better than to try . . .'?

Or is there a way of being with ourselves and our

63

disappointment that enables us to retain our equilibrium, our good humour? Humour as in 'state of mind'. And humour as in 'the capacity to appreciate the comic or amusing'.

Humour is one of the defining characteristics of being human. (Animals don't laugh, though they may have moods.) Fyodor Dostoyevsky, whose novels laid bare the intricate psychology of the human mind decades before Freud, once wrote: 'If you wish to glimpse inside a human soul and get to know a man . . . just watch him laugh. If he laughs well, he's a good man.' But what does it mean, to 'laugh well'?

Perhaps it's easier to say what it isn't. It isn't about using laughter in a situation so that you won't have to, or can't bear to, feel something else. Like shame or embarrassment, sadness or anger, grief or excitement or anxiety. Of course we all do use humour in exactly these situations, as a way of covering up these more difficult or direct forms of self-expression. But I think that to 'laugh well' is not about using laughter or humour as a substitute for another feeling. It is not a movement *away* from something, but *towards* something.

Connectedness

When the floods came, the rabbi was stranded in his house. Firemen arrived in a small boat, to find him standing knee deep in water. 'Come on,' they called, 'the river will keep on rising. You should leave with us.' 'No,' said the rabbi, 'God will protect me.' And he sent them away.

When the rains kept falling and the river kept rising, the rabbi was forced to go up to the second floor of his house. The police came by in a motor-boat: 'Come on, rabbi, there isn't much time.' 'No,' he insisted, 'I'm staying put. God will protect me.' And he sent them away.

64

Soon the rabbi is forced to stand on the roof of his house. But when the Army arrives in a large boat and tells him that the river is sure to keep on rising, the rabbi again demurs: 'All my life I have had faith. I'm going to stay. God will protect me.' And he sends them away.

And the river rises, and the rabbi is swept away and drowns.

The rabbi arrives in heaven, where he angrily approaches the throne of God: 'How can you have let this happen to me?' he demands. 'All my life I followed your laws, I did what you asked, I trusted in you to protect me. Why?'

From the throne a voice responds: 'You *schmuck*, I sent three boats.'

Jokes that need explaining, or a commentary, lose their appeal. That's the point of jokes. They are social. Laughing at the same things, sharing a sense of humour, makes you feel closer to those who 'get it'. Jokes are devices for inducing intimacy. Laughing well moves us towards intimacy, towards the realisation of that deep longing in us for connectedness to another human being. Sharing humour can satisfy the earliest hopes in us that we are not alone, and that we can give something to another person that makes a difference to them. That *we* make a difference. That we are worthwhile.

Even when we laugh alone, in that moment of pleasure when something in us is touched into humour, we are implicitly connecting with that deeper sense of ourselves which is capable of being delighted, surprised, entertained, amused by the idiosyncrasies of life. As if life were there for us to connect to. Life's openness, availability, met by our openness, our capacity to relate from the heart, or soul, or however we might choose to describe that uniqueness that we know (though fear to know) as our self.

So the jokes and humour that give rise to 'laughing well' are not substitutes for connectedness, but vehicles for it. They are communal acts, speaker and listener entering into a world of shared feeling. But this means that, often and inevitably, humour is also collusive: there are those inside the world of shared feeling and there are those outside it. Many jokes depend on this. Racist, sexist, nationalist, religious humour can depend upon the affinity of an 'us' set up against a 'them'. This makes us uncomfortable. Our principles may well be at odds with our preferences, our conscious morality with our deeper passions.

We may find ourselves in a dilemma: if we take ourselves too seriously as needing to be all of a piece, we end up not laughing at what we nevertheless find funny. What are we to do? Do we try to suppress our inconsistencies? Do we ignore them? Or do we celebrate them, laugh at them? Perhaps self-irony is a not inconsiderable gift of the human spirit: a generosity towards ourselves which allows us space to be multiple, that grants us the inner freedom to inhabit the many disparate parts of ourselves that constitute who we really are.

Yiddish

At the risk of confirming the view that jokes which need a commentary risk losing their appeal, I want to ask the following: did the story about the rabbi and the boats need its concluding Yiddishism? I could have told the joke with an anglicised version of the punchline: 'You *jerk* [or *fool*], I sent three boats.' This would have enabled readers of whatever background – unless your temperament happens to be dourly fundamentalistic – just to enjoy the sly theological/ homiletical 'moral' of the joke, the underlying polemic against a certain kind of naïve, simplistic and self-righteous piety. You could have been amused by the paradoxical notion of an anthropomorphised God using demotic English vernacular speech to put over the point that (Biblical miracles notwithstanding) the divine may become manifest in the most unlikely of shapes and forms but won't appear in the form of a personalised cosmic wizard. If you were so inclined, you might even feel enlivened by the joke's speculative spiritual perspective.

But by using the Yiddish word *schmuck* I doubtless prevented some readers feeling undividedly included in the joke's imaginative terrain. The problem is not that the joke is about a rabbi – because you could easily substitute a priest, vicar or even imam without doing (much) damage to the joke's humour and without sacrificing your appreciation of it – but that the punchline as it stands depends for its full effectiveness on your degree of connection to the ethnically particular world from which the Yiddish term *schmuck* emerges.

For part of the slyness of the joke is that *schmuck* means 'penis' as well as 'fool'. The nearest English equivalent then would probably be 'prick' or 'dickhead'. 'You dickhead, I sent three boats' would also have been funny (it might even have been funnier), with the added benefit of the shock value. But as it stands, what the joke partly depends on is the complicity between the joke teller and the putative audience, who share the unspoken knowledge that, of course, God's first language is Yiddish. Hebrew may be the language he uses for formal occasions and sacred literature, but at his most self-expressive he lapses into the vernacular, and allows himself access to the full range of scabrous and scatological forms of feeling available within his mother tongue.

Shifting perspectives

As well as connecting us with others – and sometimes dividing us from others, and against other parts of ourself – what humour and jokes also seem to do at their best is to provide us with imaginative space. Space within ourselves from which to look at the world from different perspectives, to see the world from other points of view.

During one of the annual celebrations in Red Square, Stalin suddenly held up his hand to still the cheering crowds. Waving a piece of paper he exclaimed: 'Comrades! A most historic event! A telegram of apology from Trotsky!' And he read it out: 'You were right. I was wrong. You should be leader. I should apologise. Trotsky.' And once more the crowd cheered wildly.

Stalin was about to sit down when he saw a little old man gesturing to him from the front of the crowd: 'Comrade Stalin, Comrade Stalin!' Stalin leaned down from the podium and the old man said: 'Pardon me, Comrade Stalin, but I think you may not have read the telegram quite correctly.' Stalin hushed the crowds once more: 'Comrades! Here is a simple worker, a loyal Communist, but he is telling me I have not read the telegram correctly! Come up here, comrade, you read this historic message.'

The old man went up to the podium, cleared his throat and said, 'Comrade Stalin, I think Comrade Trotsky's message is this: "*You* were right?! *I* was wrong?! *You* should be leader? *I* should *apologise*?!? . . ." '

As they say, it's *how* you tell them that counts. The particular nuances of a spoken language are hard to convey in print. And the subtleties of feeling within the Yiddish language are especially difficult to render into English. But one can see from this emblematic story that we are dealing here with a distinctive style of thinking. And it's one which I believe has something of value to offer beyond the confines of a Yiddish-speaking audience, because the anti-authoritarian thrust of much Yiddish humour is paradigmatic of the spiritual potential of all our best humour. It encourages us not to be stuck within a rigid or narrow-minded or one-dimensional way of thinking, not to isolate ourselves within an atrophied, attenuated part of ourselves. It encourages us to be vulnerable, to be expansive, to inhabit more of our self, ourselves, our multiplicity.

And perhaps it can even prolong our days. There is now

some scientific evidence that not only does laughter reduce our levels of stress, it may even protect us against cancers and heart attacks. *Alevai* ('I wish', 'I hope') we should live long enough to find out.

On Cup Final day a man makes his way to his seat, right next to the halfway line. He notices that the seat next to him is empty, leans across the space and asks his neighbour if someone will be sitting there. 'No,' says the neighbour, 'it's empty.'

'Incredible,' says the man. 'Who in their right mind would have a seat like this for the Cup Final and not use it?' 'Well, actually,' his neighbour says, 'the seat belongs to me. I was supposed to come here with my wife, but she passed away. This is the first Cup Final we've missed since we married, in 1967.'

'Oh, I'm sorry to hear that. That's terrible. But couldn't you find someone else, a friend or relative, or even a neighbour, to take the seat?'

The man shakes his head: 'No. They're all at the funeral.'

Illness

Pumpkin seeds

I was eating a rather exotic dish containing rice and
pumpkin seeds. Earlier that day I had spoken on the phone
to my son who was spending his pre-university year in Israel.
He was ill in bed, he said, with a sore throat and cold. I was
sympathetic: a couple of days before he had been in a bar
on a Saturday night in Jerusalem when two suicide bombers
had killed ten other teenagers in the bar next door. He told
me that his feeling of invincibility had gone. He'd been very
shaken, and now, on top of it, he had these symptoms. No

coincidence, I thought: how often we become ill when there is too much anxiety, or discontent, or hardship to bear.

This is a commonplace of psychoanalytic thinking: when a practical or emotional situation we find ourselves in is too demanding, too pressing, too complex for us to process psychologically within ourselves, something has to take the strain. Sometimes it's our minds which carry the can: 25 per cent of us report that we are suffering from depression or anxiety. One-fifth of the UK population are on anti-depressants. We may be aware of what is troubling us, or we may not. Either way we suffer, mentally and emotionally.

But more often than not it is our bodies which carry the excess worry, discomfort, distress. Diseases, illnesses, aches and pains express the otherwise inexpressible. Our symptoms are messages – to ourselves, to others – that we need help. Our psychic pain is translated into a language that demands attention. Physical illnesses, pains, diseases and all the minor ailments to which we are prone speak of our suffering, our tribulations, our dis-ease. And that of course leads to more distress, more suffering: a vicious cycle.

Musing on this over my supper, I found that something had caught in my throat. It felt as if a pumpkin seed had lodged there. Impossible, I thought, but as the evening wore on it felt as if the back of my throat was scarred. It was uncomfortable. No, worse: it hurt. I gargled with salt water. I took some painkillers. I went to bed. It still hurt.

As I lay there, bemoaning my sore throat – it felt as if the localised discomfort was spreading – I made the connection. I was so concerned about my son, so identified with what he was experiencing, that I was suffering his symptoms. I was unconsciously absorbed into and fused with his emotional and physical unease and discomfort. I hadn't known what to do with my feelings about his situation. I hadn't known what to do with my anxiety and my helplessness. So I'd pushed it out of my mind for the rest of the day. But in the evening it pushed its way back into me, into my body. As these newly arriving thoughts and feelings filled me up I swallowed hard. And I found that my throat was no longer sore. In fact I couldn't work out where the discomfort had been.

It seemed that once I had given enough psychological space to what I had previously had to 'swallow down' during the day – which was obviously causing me much more upset than I'd realised – I was released from its spell. Almost like magic. Except that, like all the best magic, we can't quite see how it works. Though we appreciate its effects. Once I'd made conscious the full extent of my concerns I could fall asleep. Paradoxically, by allowing myself to worry I didn't have to worry so much. On that night at least there were no black hours. My body's state had been the clue to the dilemma I didn't know I was trying to solve.

Alternatives

Many doctors report that their surgeries are full of patients suffering from psychosomatic complaints: a proliferation of backaches and chest pains and tension in the neck. But how many doctors have sufficient time to find out who is on their patients' backs? and what is the source of the heartache? and who is the pain in the neck? When we suffer from physical ill-health it is very real and immediate and demanding. How difficult it is to be with illness and pain for long enough to see if our symptoms reveal an innate physiological problem which needs caring attention and careful treatment. Or whether, like a message sent in a bottle, our bodies are being used by our symptoms to convey to our conscious minds a message about something inwardly disturbing us. Something we do need to pay more attention to, but as yet don't want to, or can't. Because it would mean we'd have to confront some difficult situation, or person. Or we'd have to change the way we live. Or we'd have to come to terms with our feelings of powerlessness, or our fear, or our disappointment, or our mortality, or any one of a host of dilemmas which are part of the fabric of the human condition.

No wonder we take our ailments and illnesses to be sorted out by someone else. And if conventional medicine is unable to fix us, then we can always turn to 'alternative' medicine. The UK now has more alternative health practitioners (homeopaths, naturopaths, reflexologists, healers, herbalists, acupuncturists and so on) than GPs. Many of these practices claim to be based on forms of ancient wisdom and a knowledge of how our bodies function, how we function, which orthodox medicine is said to have ignored or overridden.

The language of complementary health is often spiritually tinged and quite seductive: the claim to work 'holistically', to treat the 'whole' person, to help us achieve 'balance' and 'harmony'. Even though orthodox medicine is the fruit of rigorous scientific research and methodology and has transformed the quality of our lives over the last century, it is hard pressed to compete with the sub-religious appeal of harmony, balance and wholeness.

In spite of our dependence on everything from antibiotics to keyhole surgery, we seem to be living within a culture suffering from a growing disenchantment with a world governed by the scientific. A disillusionment with a world that tries to explain everything but solves so little. Although we sense the potential of science to transform the quality of our lives, we fear that something's gone wrong, something's missing, something's been lost along the way. So we seek out alternatives to the conventional materialist world, search out help which does not depend on logic and reason alone.

Illness presents us with choices. Either we become dependent on others to 'sort us out', and we grow demanding and petulant when they can't cure us. As if we had a right to be well. Or we become rather omnipotent in our thinking and start to believe that if only we did 'X' or thought 'Y' we should be able to cure ourselves, or render ourselves immune from the inevitable limitations our bodies place upon us. Or we search for a 'spiritual' response to our lack of health and end up losing something else: our capacity for critical thinking, our ability to differentiate between the rational and the irrational. As G. K. Chesterton once remarked, when we cease to believe in God we will not believe in nothing, we will believe in anything.

Once our trust in science goes, the soul still hungers for security. But if you suspend your discriminating intelligence you can and will believe in whatever you want to believe: God's name appears in vegetables to rejuvenate the sick, statues bleed and enable the lame to walk, cancer can be cured by healing hands.

Illness is not only physical and emotional – grievous as these kinds of illness are. We can succumb too to an illness of the spirit. We lose our rigour of thought and elevate the irrational and all manner of mumbo-jumbo to pride of place within our thinking.

The power of the mind

Yet it seems that a delicate balancing exercise is required. For it is becoming clearer that our bodies may have more scope to heal and maintain themselves than we might at first imagine. With an increasingly sedentary and ageing population in the West, the medical establishment is beginning to join with the 'alternative' practitioners in asking if it is possible to harness the body's own potential in order to help us prevent illnesses like heart disease and diabetes. And if lack of exercise and poor eating habits have debilitating effects on our well-being, can changing our diets and finding enjoyable forms of exercise help the body's own self-healing? Are allergies and asthma attacks an inevitable by-product of contemporary life? Or can changes in how we live our lives – and how we think about our lives and our priorities – make a difference?

There is an ever-growing body of scientifically based evidence that certain kinds of illnesses and ill-health are susceptible to amelioration in unexpected ways. People who 'think positively' do seem to have better immunity – in relation to cancer, for example – than those who don't, or can't. (The left side of the brain is responsible for strengthening immunity and is also the area of the brain responsible for active thinking. And it can be activated by visualisation techniques.) One in three infertile couples suffer from no recognisable medical problem: unconscious fears (which can be accessed, with help) seem to prevent conception. And the 'placebo effect' is well attested: in some situations dud pills are as effective as proper treatment.

The mind is an immensely powerful tool. It is a spiritual resource. Of course there are no guarantees: emotional and social and environmental factors are always present to complicate the picture, to subvert our best intentions. Nevertheless, although the mind is never under our control – though we live with the illusion that it is, more or less – we may be able to utilise our thinking to a greater degree than perhaps we have been brought up to believe.

Prayer

Even more surprising, perhaps, is the scientific evidence for the power of prayer. In an experiment in 1988 in the US, 393 patients admitted over ten months to a coronary care unit were randomly assigned to an intercessory prayer group and to a control group. The first group were prayed for by participating Christians praying outside the hospital. The control group were not. What happened? The control group required ventilatory assistance, antibiotics and diuretics significantly more frequently than the patients in the first group. Over the years this type of experiment has been repeated, with variations, in different countries and with patients suffering from other illnesses. Although there are the inevitable post-trial disagreements about the significance of the statistics gathered, the groups prayed for are consistently reported to have suffered less, or recovered faster, than the control groups.

Evidence for the superiority of the Christian God? I don't think so. But something is happening here which goes beyond the boundaries of our current understanding of how our world works, how we are interconnected with one another (or can be), how the material and the spiritual (for want of a better word) dimensions of existence interrelate. How mind, body and spirit hold together.

We know only too well how suddenly, in the midst of life, our lives can be turned upside down. We may find ourselves (or a loved one) having to live with cancer, or a tumour, or Aids, or the effects of a stroke. There may be anger, confusion, fear, as well as the disruption and the pain. 'Why is this happening?' we wonder. 'What have I done wrong?' Plagued as we are by doubts, the questions tumble out and we find ourselves thinking about the resources we have, and need. Can religious faith make a difference? Or the quality of the loving care we receive? Can anything make a difference, help us live with the hardship, the heartache, the knowledge that pain and illness and loss shadow us till the end of our days?

We are a puzzle to ourselves. The mystery of our being adheres to that lump of grey matter we call our brain. What spiritual perspective is possible in the midst of this disorder?

Do we turn to the neurologist and writer Oliver Sacks? 'I think the wonder of our aesthetic or religious sense is increased by the fact that it depends on three pounds of jelly in our head . . . I've never been able to imagine any sort of personal god, but I think one wants to say there's a divine order and beauty about the world.'

Or do we turn to the prophet Jeremiah, who finds himself crying out to his God in words filled simultaneously with both hope and defiance? 'Heal me, Eternal One, and I shall be healed. Save me and I shall be saved. For you are my praise' (17:14).

Or can we gain sustenance from both?

Justice

Judging others, judging ourselves

One of the most common criticisms of spirituality is that it is self-centred. As it becomes increasingly fashionable to parade one's spiritual interests – whether it is Richard Gere's dalliance with the Dalai Lama or Madonna's flirtation with Kabbalah or Cherie Blair's sporting of a crystal pendant – so the cry of self-indulgence is raised. This designer spirituality is seen as just another manifestation of our culture of narcissism: spirituality 'lite' for the Me generation.

Nevertheless, two thousand years ago the rabbinic sage Hillel taught a simple rule-of-thumb: 'Do not judge your fellow human being until you have been in their place.' On first reading this aphorism sounds like a rebuke: a warning against our knowingness. Our unthinking belief that we know how others might experience the world and feel about their lives. Our assumptions about how they should behave. The message seems to be: back off, suspend your judgement of others. Their circumstances are not the same as yours, so who are you to judge their actions?

But on closer examination, I think we can also read Hillel's dictum as an invitation. A summons to inhabit, imaginatively, what it is like to be in someone else's skin. An appeal to our capacity for fellow feeling, for a recognition of a shared humanity. And through that recognition, an empathic realisation of how hard it is for any human being to live up to their best intentions. How often we fall short of what we aspire to be. How often we fail to do justice to ourselves.

Undoubtedly, seeking a spiritual dimension to life can be selfish, solipsistic. Giving ourselves good feelings about our sensitivity. Giving ourselves a tingle of self-congratulation about being deeper or wiser or more balanced than others. Giving ourselves a frisson of excitement as we play with ideas about esoteric forces and energy fields, thrilling ourselves towards enlightenment. Such spirituality is like masturbating our soul into the self-gratifying delusory state of feeling special, climaxing with the becoming flush of moral superiority.

But as I understand it, spirituality involves an intercourse with the world. How we act with each other – with family, friends, strangers, and particularly with those whom we experience as *different from us* – is the prism through which the integrity of our spiritual life can be judged.

Practical spirituality

The Hebrew Bible's prescription for the social ordering of society depended above all on one quality: justice. Threaded through the ancient texts, the demand for justice as a guiding principle for personal and community life was no abstract requirement. It was not a pious hope – or not only a pious hope. It was a declaration of intent. The creators of the Hebraic vision felt themselves part of a people called to live as an exemplary presence in the world. Everyday life was to be governed by detailed laws for the economic, social, sexual, cultural and moral behaviour of a people. The vision was magnificent, inspired, inspirational. And daunting, intimidating.

As time passed, the gap that will always exist between ideals and reality became increasingly apparent. People who had been asked to surpass themselves, to rise above their innate human foibles and weaknesses and submit to the stringencies of a supposedly divine plan, found the task beyond them. Nevertheless, prophetic voices found themselves urging the Israelite community not to abandon the vision but to renew the search for ways of enacting the highest ideals which had been set before them. 'It has been shown to you what is good, and what the Eternal seeks from you,' says Micah, 'is it not to do justly, and love goodness, and walk humbly with your God?' (6:8). The only justification for the continued survival of this small, insignificant near-Eastern tribe came to be seen as their adherence to this particular way of being-in-the-world.

That Jews subsequently earned the reputation for legalism is a harsh judgement on that vision. They were engaged in an extraordinary attempt to inculcate justice into daily interpersonal behaviour: relations between men and women, parents and children, workers and employers, humans and animals, people and the land; rules of property and inheritance, health and disease, judges and witnesses; obligations in regard to education, charity, family, strangers, the elderly, the marginalised; relations with other nations. An entire framework for life founded on the human capacity for justice.

The Hebrew word for justice, *tzedek*, was refracted into the word for 'charitable giving to others', *tzedakah*. 'Charity' was not dependent on feelings. It was about right action: acting justly in relation to others in order to help create a God-willed harmony in the human realm. This was to be a model for all humanity. The vagaries and contingencies of life might erode the vision of how things could be, but each individual had it within his or her grasp to help repair the fabric of family, community, society. Everyday life was the forum in which *tikkun olam* (the repair of the world) was to be enacted. This was practical spirituality – the daily noble path to the amelioration of the world.

It was (is) a breathtaking, grandiose vision, a humble and arrogant dream. From Micah to Marx, and beyond, the millennia-old call for the righteous ordering of personal and societal relations has infiltrated its way into the foundations of modern consciousness. And justice is still delayed, and still desired, and still resisted, and still dreamed: just beyond our grasp, elusive, achievable in parts and at moments, before it is once more eclipsed by personal and collective forces frightened by the demand that we transcend our pettiness, our narrowness, our selfishness, and act towards others as we would have them act towards us.

Justice and mercy

One of the second-century founders of rabbinic Judaism, Simeon ben Gamliel, used to say that 'On three things does the world rest: on truth, on justice, and on peace.' That civilisation could be preserved only through adherence to these fundamental values was a defiant statement of hope in the face of the collective pain of a people whose world had disappeared. The Romans had occupied Palestine and pulled down the Temple, the centre of Hebraic cultic worship. It was left to the following generations of scholars to revivify the ancient vision, to find new ways to incarnate the spiritual values of old. They realised that love cannot be ordered; but justice, to some extent, can.

They looked back at the Biblical texts and saw how the qualities of justice and mercy had always been interwoven in the legislation and narratives of their tradition. They saw

81

too that these qualities were, inevitably, in tension with each other. Justice requires dispassionate judgement; mercy involves compassionate judgement. We each have a capacity to be detached, objective, able to weigh up situations without an over-close personal identification, without letting our feelings unduly influence our thinking. And of course we also have the capacity for a loving, generous, forgiving, empathetic response to events and situations.

The co-existence within us of these different human qualities influenced how these rabbis thought about God. They saw that there were two major names for God within the Hebrew texts: the tetragrammaton YHVH, *Adonai*; and the plural noun *Elohim* (see chapter on You). And they projected these dual aspects of themselves on to these names. When *Elohim* appeared in the texts, they suggested that this was God representing the quality of justice. When *Adonai* appeared, it was God's attributes of love and mercy that were being evoked.

The rabbis created homilies to explain how the qualities of justice and mercy co-exist within the divine being, and by extension within the world:

> It's like a king who had empty containers. He said: 'If I put hot water into them they will crack; if I put icy water into them they will contract.' So what did the king do? He mixed the hot with the cold and poured the mixture into the containers, and they endured. Similarly, God said: 'If I create the world only with the attribute of mercy, people will feel free to sin as much as they want. But if I create it only with the attribute of strict justice, how could the world survive? Behold, I will create it with both attributes. Would that it might endure!'

This juxtaposition of compassion and strictness informs current debates about the just ordering of societies. We are offered the liberal view that individuals are social creatures and that justice requires universal rules protecting the individual, including their freedom from harm and want. And we have the conservative view that justice cannot be created from coercive legislation (on taxation, welfare, regulation, anti-discrimination practice, state interference in financial/market initiatives, etc.), a view which places a higher premium on individual autonomy than on compassion.

Our own spiritual development takes place within this wider debate about how we order society. We may try to escape into a private, narcissistic world of spiritual discovery, but that means losing connection with a basic component of the Judaeo-Christian spiritual heritage. For as the Bible emphasises time and again, it is in our relation to other human beings that our relationship to the divine is enacted. Justice is not about our kindness, but about our recognition that others have a claim on us by virtue of a shared humanity. The Talmud puts it with pithy directness: 'Love God in those He has created.'

Divine justice, human justice

But what about God? God's so-called 'justice'? Integral to traditional theologies – Jewish, Christian, Islamic – is the image of a divine being who acts justly. And yet bad things keep on happening to good people. Murders, rapes, earthquakes, robberies, diseases, disasters and accidents, large-scale and individual. An endless list. Where is the justice? At every moment another victim, another blow to the vision of a just ordering of life. How can one speak of God's justice? An old question.

The Talmudic rabbis imagined a prayer that God repeats to himself, daily: 'May it be that my attribute of mercy outweighs my attribute of strict justice.' For they knew they had a problem: timeless scepticism about reconciling human suffering and divine justice. Memorably, the Book of Job had questioned traditional 'explanations' of suffering. Its eventual pained acknowledgement that there are experiences which can never be understood or explained made this book a crucial counterbalance to some of the apparent certainties of monotheistic thinking. Job refuses to submit to the platitudes of the past, to the conventional theology of his friends and their attempts to defend a perfect God. He is forced into a personal confrontation with the deepest questions about the meaning of life. Other people's answers will not do. He has to engage with life in all its quixotic strangeness, and wrestle from it a meaning for himself alone.

Job's new understanding emerges near the end of the book, when he acknowledges that his previous ideas about how justice works have now been contradicted by his own fraught personal experience: 'I had heard of you [God] only by ear; but now my eye sees you' (42:5). His suffering forces him to acknowledge that the world is not ordered as he wishes it to be. It is freighted in mystery. What comes into being is saturated in uncertainty, indeterminacy, unknownness. Justice doesn't just happen. It isn't just given. If it is to exist at all, it has to be constructed – by us.

And in what spirit? A spirit of humility, it seems: 'I melt away, I repent in dust and ashes' (42:6). Recognising our fragility – our transience and our limitations – enables us to recognise the needs of others. We are all in the same boat. We need each other. The choice is stark: we can drown in despair, flooded by the injustices of the world. Or we can float free of our inhibitions and inhabit the ancient vision anew, allowing compassion to overcome self-centredness and pursuing justice with a divine determination. Justice: empathy in action; justice: a surging effervescence of human concern. 'Let justice roll down like waters, and righteousness like a mighty stream . . .' (Amos 5:24).

Kabbalah

God is everything that exists, though everything that exists is not God.

Moses Cordovero, 1522–70

At each place, in each hour, in each act, in each speech, the holy can blossom forth . . . Man cannot approach the divine by reaching beyond the human; he can approach Him through becoming human . . .

Martin Buber

The search for paradise

By rights, if you are female you should stop reading this now. Or if you are under forty. Or if you're single. That is the tradition I grew up with. The Kabbalah – the Jewish mystical tradition in all its variegated and esoteric richness – could be studied only by married men over the age of forty. This ancient hidden wisdom was to be revealed solely to select male individuals through a process of individual oral transmission from teacher to student. Maturity of years and the solidity of family life were the prerequisites for advanced exploration into the mysteries of the universe. So what happened?

How is it that for today's Hollywood celebrity in search of enlightenment, yoga and Zen have given way to Kabbalah? That on both sides of the Atlantic audiences pack into meeting-halls, synagogues, seminar rooms in search of Jewish mysticism's answers to life's questions? And that only a minority of these seekers are Jewish? How is it that Kabbalah – the word means 'that which has been received' – has become a fad, a must-have spiritual accessory, the Armani of alternative spiritual practices?

The contemporary popularization of the Kabbalah is a complex socio-historical phenomenon. One can trace it back to the opening decades of the twentieth century and Martin Buber's explorations into Hasidism, the mass revivalist movement that had dominated eighteenth- and nineteenth-century eastern European Jewish life. He translated Hasidic teaching and lore from Yiddish into German and transmuted its Kabbalistically inspired philosophy and ethos into a narrative form that made it accessible to a Western secular audience.

Although Buber's evangelizing work eventually gained an enthusiastic following in the English-speaking world, his idiosyncratic reading of Hasidic ideas had its critics. Foremost among them was Gershom Scholem, professor of Jewish mysticism at the Hebrew University, Jerusalem, whose academic life was devoted to rescuing the Kabbalah from the scorn of previous generations of scholars who had refused to see Jewish mystical literature as worthy of intellectual study and research. But while Scholem demonstrated how Kabbalistic practice had always been rooted in Jewish legalism and ritual life, the antinomian spirit in Buber led him to strive to rescue the living kernel of spiritual and sacred truth from the husk of a rabbinical world view which he considered of lesser value, and even an impediment to 'true' spiritual life.

Yet both these figures have contributed to the current popularity of Kabbalah. Buber's influence was perhaps predominantly among non-Jews. His retelling of Hasidic stories highlighted the individual seeker after truth; and his emphasis on ecstasy, the body, silence, dreams, visions, the quest for individuation, fed into the 1960s counterculture with its interest in alternative forms of spiritual teaching. The Beatles' flirtation with the Maharishi was symptomatic of this sea-change in popular Western engagement with previously unavailable spirituality. Anything other than the safe, worn-out pieties of monotheism.

The last decades of the twentieth century saw a further cultural shift away from rationalism, scientism, and traditional religious answers towards holistic and New Age beliefs, and a veritable marketplace of spiritual practices drawn from around the world and embracing both ancient tribal cultures as well as newly packaged forms of traditional Eastern religions like Buddhism and Hinduism. And Gershom Scholem's pupils and disciples played their part in this. Their readily digestible translations and anthologies make the convoluted and sometimes baffling erudition of the Jewish mystical tradition accessible to all. Although they were addressing a predominantly Jewish audience, there has been a huge cross-fertilization of ideas in recent decades. The postmodernist ethos of mix'n'match has meant that the Kabbalah – in both its Buber- and Scholem-inspired guises – is now freely available for the use of any seeker after spiritual truth.

The dangers of paradise

The Talmud narrates a short, cryptic tale: 'Our rabbis taught: Four entered *Pardes* (the orchard) – Ben Azzai, Ben Zoma, Aher, and Rabbi Akiva. Ben Azzai looked and died. Ben Zoma looked and went mad. Aher cut the shoots. Rabbi Akiva emerged in peace.' What's going on here?

Pardes (the orchard) refers to **paradise**: see my Introduction. To 'enter the orchard' means to approach 'paradise' by engaging in mystical speculation and practices. So our story tells of four scholars venturing beyond the first three 'levels' of truth (**p**lain meanings, **r**eminders, **d**eepening one's insight) into new intellectual and emotional and spiritual terrain: **s**ecret knowledge. But it warns that exploring esoteric or mystical knowledge can take us into confusing and hazardous territory. It can result in death; or madness; or cutting oneself off from one's roots. (The story uses the derogatory nickname Aher – 'the other one' – for Rabbi Elisha ben Avuyah, who cut himself off from his Judaic heritage and became a heretic.) Only Akiva retained his composure and found a way of integrating his new understandings into his daily life.

This ancient parable highlights the hazards (as well as the attraction) of exploring spirituality. Not everyone can handle what they find. Pursuing all the answers to life's mysteries – to the unanswerable questions about good and evil, hope and despair, life and death and our purpose on earth – can lead to the death of old ways of thinking and feeling; it can stimulate you more than you can bear; it can cut you off from family and friends. Not all of this may be unwelcome. But it should give one pause for thought.

The thrill of privileged access to ideas previously shrouded in secrecy can make one unduly susceptible to bogus claims and spurious insights. It can be a glamorous, self-deluding cover for ersatz and superficial panaceas offering 'self-awareness', 'self-realization', 'self-fulfilment': fraudulent nonsense which seduces you into a cosy glow of self-absorption. Self-discovery in bite-sized, pre-packaged globules of self-serving 'wisdom'. 'Finding oneself' as a modish disguise for selfishness.

DIY spirituality sells. Kabbalah courses are full. Booksellers' shelves brim with new titles. Is this book any different? Of course I would like to think so. But I acknowledge my scepticism about much popular writing about spirituality, and Kabbalah in particular. What was once integrated into a devotional life has now become a substitute for it. It's not that I agree with the previous restrictions on those who wished to study Judaism's more esoteric understandings. Such restrictions were paternalistic and often patriarchal. Ideas about a spiritual dimension to everyday life should be available and accessible to all – regardless of faith, age, gender, status.

But I also believe that spirituality is not an alternative to a life of ethical reflectiveness. Nor is it a substitute for failures in emotional relatedness. Although it can help us engage more fully with life, it does not provide comprehensive answers to the mysteries of life. Although it may help us refine our sensitivity to the mystery, the contingency, the sheer strangeness of our being – and our being here at this time and in this place – it is not an end in itself.

The Kabbalah teaches that spirituality involves service: becoming more human so that through the gateway of the everyday world we can recognise the interconnectedness of all being, and thereby recognise that the world awaits us. Needs us. 'You can mend the cosmos by any action you choose to do . . .' (Isaac Luria, 1534–72). If developing our spiritual self-awareness does not lead to a development in our awareness of the needs of others, the needs of the world, we have failed.

Entering the orchard

Imagine finding a map of consciousness. A map on which you could trace the currents of feeling and thinking that course through your body and mind moment by moment. A map on which you could plot your moods, your highs and lows of energy and desire. A map with which you could transform confusion into clarity, lethargy into liveliness, depression into delight, pain into pleasure, isolation into involvement and interrelationship. The Kabbalists believed they had access to such knowledge: maps of being which helped join up our inner life with the life of the world. Our being with the being of the universe.

They imagined a tree, which was a ladder, which was a human body. They pictured energy flowing up and down, from the roots in the ground to the tops of the branches, from the earth to the heavens, from the soles of our feet to the crowns of our head. And back again. Energy flowing through and down, from the heights to the depths, from above to below, from the infinite to the here and now. And back again. A constant movement of being. Our being. The being of the universe. Our being in the universe. The universe being in us.

Like the Hindu concept of the *chakras*, the Kabbalistic map had energy centres. Ten *sefirot*, emanations, centres of psychic gravity, which one could reflect upon to enter into paradise. Paradise: what life presents to you moment by moment. This 'Tree of Life' – cast in the form of the human body, which represents a map of all human being, which reflects a map of all divine being – traced sacred pathways between the *sefirot*.

What were the psycho-spiritual elements of this map of consciousness, map of life, map of being?

We start with our feet on the ground . . . rooted, grounded in the physical world is *malchut*, the material *kingdom*: the world of paying the bills, negotiating the traffic, doing the washing up . . . how well does our energy flow within this domain? whose other name is *shechinah*, God's immanent (female) *presence* . . .

. . . from where we move up the tree, the body, to the genitals and the reproductive system: *yesod*, the *foundation* of our sexuality, relationships, shared human feelings, intimacy, creativity . . . source of so many dramas of our personal and emotional lives . . .

. . . then, following the flow of energy, we move up and

out to a pair of *sefirot* represented by the right leg, hip and muscular system: *netzach,* the *victory* of our capacity for expansive appetites for food and drink, and all that we devour to survive in the world . . .

. . . balanced by the corresponding left leg and side: *hod,* the *splendour* of our ability to limit our desires to consume the world and what it contains . . .

generating   expanding   contracting
our energy moves through these three lower *sefirot* . . . to the torso, chest and lungs and heart: *tiferet,* our appreciation of *beauty* . . . aesthetic, mental, emotional, spiritual receptivity . . . the centre of our being . . .

. . . and so we move up to the right arm and hand, *hesed,* our capacity for *love,* how we act towards others, with compassion, with decency, with empathy . . . our openness to others, and ourselves . . .

. . . balanced by *gevurah,* the *strength* to say no, the ability to set limits, to judge dispassionately: left hand and arm . . . how well do we move between selflessness and self-awareness? something else is required, further up the Tree, the body . . .

. . . *hochmah,* right side of the brain, the *wisdom* of intuition, moments of insight, clarity, sparks of spiritual discernment . . .

. . . and also *binah,* left side of the brain, *understanding*, the ability to think, remember, analyse, evaluate with intellectual discrimination . . .

. . . and so to the tenth of the *sefirot,* the highest place of our inner world, our being, which is also the being of the world: *keter,* the *crown* of our heads, the gateway to the transcendent, to the God who is everything (and thereby flows through all the *sefirot*) . . . who is also known in the Kabbalah as *ayin,* that is *Nothing* . . . the divine as everything is *Nothing* we can encompass with our minds . . . we reach the crown of our knowing: flashes of revelation, moments of meaning, moments of meeting . . .

Nothing, more to say . . .

A health warning

Reading this chapter on the Kabbalah is the spiritual equivalent of going to a restaurant and trying to eat the menu.

Love

She was calling to say goodbye. There was really only one thing for her to say, those three words that all the terrible art, the worst pop songs and movies, the most seductive lies, can somehow never cheapen. I love you. She said it over and again before the line went dead. And that is what they were all saying down their phones, from the hijacked planes and the burning towers. There is only love, and then oblivion.

Ian McEwan, novelist, 15 September 2001

. . . love always exposes one's incompetence.

Adam Phillips, psychoanalyst

Paradise gained, paradise lost

Love haunts our lives. The search for it, the struggle to hold on to it, the memory of it, the reminders of its absence. From the earliest moments of our lives we are bound up within a drama of passion and longing as we strive to be held and fed, to feel warm and secure, to feel that all is well with the world and with oneself, who is the world. Long before we have the words for it, this is what it means to be loved. Something larger than ourselves sustains us, nurtures us, protects us: we receive what we need.

Then we learn – slowly, over time – that we can give as well as take. What we've been given when things go well – a sense of plenitude and worth – activates our desire to return the gift. And this is how we learn to love. We learn to smile, we learn to stroke, we learn to interact and play. What flows from us produces a response and, amazingly, more of what we like and need comes back. We give out love through giving out our needs, and love flows back, a self-renewing cycle of interrelationship: taking in the goodness, then moving out into the world, connecting to it with our growing sense that we can make pleasurable things happen because we have something of value in us, something appreciated, something enjoyable, loved and loveable. Our selves.

This intense, prolific process through our early months, then years, becomes our prototype for love. Our template. The emotional foundations on which we build our subsequent relationships. But here the drama darkens. Because, firstly and inevitably, in our earliest relationships there are frustrations and failures and gaps in provision. There can be carelessness, indifference, irritation; or worse. Sometimes as infants, and later, we show too much liveliness, or inwardness, self-assertion or neediness or upset – and love seems to withdraw itself. Sometimes a mother's love can be too erratic, or intrusively demanding.

In our desperation, our own capacities for loving-through-relatedness go into eclipse: we become prematurely self-sufficient; or reckless; or cold; or destructive. We become fearful about what we want, what's inside of us, what will happen if we show our true colours, sensuality and shit and all. Who will love us now? Although we feel love's throb within us still, although we yearn to reach out in love and be loved in return, early failings impoverish us, overshadow our hopefulness. Darken love's promise.

And our drama of love darkens secondly, and tragically, because our idyllic love-in with our early protectors and nurturers is doomed to end in disappointment. For our early love is boundless. It is insatiable. There are no limits to what we would want from and with our parents. But, sadly, we have to forego the ambiguously loving embrace of those who provide that boundaryless world. It has to end in tears. Tears of sadness and rage. Tears in the fabric of unfulfillable wishfulness in which we are wrapped.

Racked by desire for oneness-with-another, in the future people will remind us, unconsciously, of our earliest loves: our mother, father, carers, siblings. Above all our parents. So we move beyond the bosom of the family in pursuit of replacements for the unobtainable lovers we once knew and possessed but did not have for ever, and could not have for ourselves alone. Unbeknown to ourselves, we search to find them again – counterparts to them, representations and embodiments of them – seeking out loving relationships that help us recreate (i.e. reinvent) our lost world, or gain mastery over it.

We learn love from what is transient. And so we are always wanting: lacking and wishing. Who will fill the gaps? The holes in us, the space between me and you. Paradise has been lost, though we never had it. The Garden of Unconditional Love – from which we have been expelled – never really existed, though we tasted its fruit.

God's love, our love

Does the emotional patterning of our early years influence our spiritual quest? Does what we learn of love (and its vicissitudes) in one domain prove proleptic, prophetic, as we (perhaps unknowingly) seek to relocate it somewhere else?

Some would say that the search for God is the attempt to re-experience the (idealised) love we once felt: an all-embracing, nurturing presence that we can rely on to protect us from harm, soothe our pains, encourage our own loving instincts to emerge in caring and compassionate ways. Or perhaps, when the failures in parental love have been too severe, one seeks God's love in order to assuage one's inner emptiness or despair. One of the traditional images of God is of a Carer who (at long last) will never let us down. Unless we let our Carer down: the sting in the tale, so to speak.

Sometimes the texts of old have God saying 'You are precious, so I will love you, regardless . . .' At other times the divine voice is more equivocal: 'Love me, then I will love you back . . .' Traditional Judaeo-Christian spirituality moves between these views. We are the beloved creation of a God whose love embraces all, endlessly. And we are in a demanding, covenantal relationship, expected to manifest love in order to merit love in return.

So if you personify God as an unconditionally benign parental force, then God's love is a mystery. We are loved because we are, and it's up to us to perceive it, give thanks for it, and in turn imitate the divine generosity in our relationships with others.

If, however, you personify God as a more exacting presence, requiring our love, then we're on trial (as we were as children). Have you been sufficiently 'good' – open-hearted or obedient or longsuffering or loving – to be found worthy of receiving God's beneficence? When God is pictured as being like a demanding parent, then failure to feel God's love means that if we try again, try harder, perhaps we will earn the love we need. But the reward may be endlessly deferred.

Over and again, traditional religious believers have had to make their accommodations with these irresolvable questions of faith. For some, the rituals of religion become gestures of love, opportunities for a willing self-surrender to traditions hallowed by the loving embrace of generations. For others, conventional religious traditions and beliefs can be experienced as a form of cruelty, God's love a sacred vehemence requiring more from us than we can or wish to give.

For much of the time though, our contemporary preoccupation with human love seems to have replaced older questions about religious love. We wonder why love seems so elusive. We wonder how to retain and nurture our capacity for love. We wonder how selfless is our love, or how manipulative, or how erotic. The drama of human love presses in on us with the same urgency once felt in relation to divine love. But though our questions may now be human-centred, at the core of our being they echo with an ancient refrain. 'Love is strong as death...' (Song of Songs 8:6): so why does love die, or never seem enough? Why does love come mixed with possessiveness, with 'jealousy cruel as the grave...' (8:6)?

The work of love

Our incompetence in love is humbling. We fumble in our confusion. We stumble over our desires. If, as the poet Philip Larkin has written, 'What will survive of us is love', where can we start? Are there fragments of traditional wisdom that can guide us, filaments of insight that retain sufficient immediacy to help us with love in everyday life?

'For one human being to love another human being: that is perhaps the most difficult task that has been entrusted to us, the ultimate task, the final test and proof, the work for which all our work is merely preparation.' The poet Rainer Maria Rilke's central European humanist seriousness is daunting. But also promising. Much influenced by Russian pietism, he sees love as work. As does his down-to-earth German-Jewish predecessor, the essayist Ludwig Boerne: 'Everyone has in their life a day when, like the first human beings in Eden, one finds love without care and trouble. But when this day is past, you earn love, as you earn bread, by the sweat of the brow.'

This is close to hand. Giving love, earning love, working at love. Does this mundane pragmatism feel disappointing? We are so used to the romanticisation and sentimentalization of love. Yet to pay attention to love as work can help rescue it from the world of emotion alone and root it in a deeper commitment, a developing spiritual practice.

Love as work is a spiritual discipline. The Hebrew word *avodah* means both 'work/burden' and 'service of God'. As we develop our capacities for love, can we transform the work of love from arduousness to ardour, from burden to service?

'Love God in the human beings the divine has created', says the Talmud. So-called 'religious' love is to be enacted between people. This echoes one of the Bible's central commands: 'Love your neighbour as yourself . . .' (Leviticus 19:18). The next words in the text are less frequently quoted: ' . . . *ani Adonai*: I am the Eternal.' Our responsibility to engage lovingly, one human being to another, is rooted in the divine energy animating all being.

Hasidic thought gave special prominence to this ancient inner connection between the human and the divine. Rabbi Mendel of Kosov (d. 1825) comments on their interrelationship. Our Levitical verse implies, he said, that '*if* a person loves their fellow, *then* the divine presence rests with them.' Active involvement in the work of love brings God into the world, so to speak. This suggests that all our relationships – with family, friends, colleagues, strangers – are potential spiritual adventures. Martin Buber expands this Hasidic ethos into a radical spiritual challenge: 'To love God truly, one must first love human beings. And if anyone tells you that they love God and do not love other people, you will know that they are lying.'

Loving others, loving ourselves

'Love your neighbour' sounds so simple. It's become a cliché. Yet we know how elusive it is in everyday life. Rabbi Moshe Leib of Sassov (d. 1807) once told his disciples that he had learned a secret about it from a conversation he'd overheard between two villagers:

'Do you love me?' asked the first.

'I love you deeply,' replied the second.

'Do you know what really hurts me?' asked the first.

'How can I know what really hurts you?' shrugged the second.

'But if you don't know what causes me pain, how can you say that you really love me?' responded the first.

'This was a profound lesson about the nature of love,' said Moshe Leib: 'No one really loves their neighbour unless they know what's hurting them.' But if we do not acknowledge the hurt within ourselves – our fragility, our vulnerability, our woundedness – we cannot bear to hear it in the other: our partner, our parent, our child; all those who cry out for justice or just cry themselves to sleep, our 'neighbour'. No one is ever loved enough.

Love is a spiritual drama on which the world depends. We can love beauty, nature, works of art, music, movies, gardening, pets, food, sex, sport, shopping – but can we love ourselves in ways which transform selfishness to selflessness? If there is indeed 'only love, and then oblivion', then the language of love should be upon our tongues and in our hearts. Not only when death calls, but in the midst of life. The alphabet of love is learnt, moment by moment, in our encounters with one another. 'Everyone is a letter in God's name.' Tongue-tied beginners, we stumble over our lessons.

Money

The love of money is the root of all evil.

1 Timothy 6

Gold is very excellent . . . it will even get a soul into Paradise.

Christopher Columbus, 1503

Money is better than poverty, if only for financial reasons.

Woody Allen

Confronting the questions

We live in a world in which less than 4 per cent of the personal wealth of the 225 richest people could give *all the poor of the world* access to basic medical and educational amenities as well as adequate nutrition. A world in which those who sit behind office desks punching keyboards are paid ten times as much as the people who clean the office toilets and a hundred times as much as those who assemble the keyboards in the Third World. Of the surplus wealth generated in the US in the last twenty years of the twentieth century, 95 per cent was appropriated and consumed by just 5 per cent of Americans.

Does the scandal of inequality render redundant any talk of spirituality? To think about economic issues from a spiritual perspective can seem like an irrelevance: the self-indulgent posturing of those fortunate enough to have material security who cannot face the harsh reality that economic deprivation needs to be addressed through the hard graft of social and political action.

Monotheistic and Eastern religions have been confronted by these questions for millennia. Is money helpful for one's spiritual life, or a hindrance to it? Can the use we make of our money – and the stance we adopt towards it – be integrated into our spiritual journey? Or does our attitude to it become idolatrous: where we value the pursuit and accumulation of wealth as an end in itself? Is the New Testament's stark dichotomy true – that in the end we cannot serve both God and Mammon?

We know that our attitude to money exists somewhere on a continuum between self-interest and selflessness. Between a desire for security, comfort, adventure, pleasure – whatever it is we believe money can buy – and a desire to achieve some further purposeful meaning in our lives. How much money we need, what we use our money for, the extent to which we use it to serve ourselves or for the good of others, our attitude towards consumerism – these are practical spiritual questions we all face. And they are questions at the core of the spiritual tradition with which I align myself: the Hebrew Bible, and the Judaic concern for stewardship, social responsibility and *tzedakah* ('charity').

Spiritual opportunities

As we saw in a previous chapter (Justice), *tzedakah* also means righteousness. Benign financial activity was seen as a spiritual opportunity as well as a moral requirement. The

101

proper use of money was part of one's devotional life. For the storyteller–legislators of the Torah – the document containing the founding narratives of the Hebrew people – poverty was an undesirable condition, not an ascetic discipline. Both the nation as a whole and the individuals within it – from lowly Israelites to the king himself – were made responsible for the welfare of economically disadvantaged members of society: the poor were grouped together with widows and orphans as needing special protection. Among other safeguards, the poor were to receive extra food from the harvest, a fair hearing in trials, and money lent without interest. This was spirituality for everyday life. Spirituality in action.

Religious behaviourism – adherence to the details of cultic and ritual life while ignoring the interpersonal dimensions of religious life – was condemned by the biblical narrators, and later by Israel's prophets, as antithetical to the intentions of *Adonai*, the spirit of all being, which they felt had chosen Israel to exemplify a particular way of being in the world. A way which saw each human being as precious, a way which recognised our rootedness in the material domain but which challenged the individual to develop a distinctive relationship to materiality, money, economic activity. 'Sharing your bread with the hungry, taking the rejected poor into your home' became a prophetic imperative (Isaiah 58:7).

The prophets were responding to a situation not so unlike our own, in which the daily exigencies of survival – the need for food, shelter, physical well-being – become so all-consuming that life becomes dominated by these needs. A world in which a human invention, money, comes to be experienced as if it has some kind of external god-like authority. A world in which people devote their lives to its pursuit, accumulate it beyond their needs, use it as the ground out of which their self-worth grows, sacrifice to it their honour, their health, their peace of mind, the well-being of their families, the well-being of their souls.

And the prophetic rejoinder to this, to the overwhelming immediacy of our needs for material security, was to articulate a form of divine pathos: to say that because the pursuit of money can break the link between our actions and their consequences, it is a spiritual necessity that financial security be accessible to all. Particularly those who do not have the wherewithal to achieve it for themselves: the disadvantaged, the downtrodden, all those suffering from economic inequality. Prophetic compassion for our human condition – creatures of flesh and blood who need food to eat, clothes to wear, homes to inhabit – was transmuted into a passion to include everyone within society as deserving the security that materialism can provide.

The stance advocated by Israel's prophets towards money and material well-being grew out of, and reflected, their religio-historical awareness. A small, unremarkable tribe with pretensions of grandeur had been freed from slavery. This was cause for celebration and thankfulness. But the recorders of that story of liberation had wondered whether in the future they would find themselves enslaved once more, this time to forces of their own making: 'When you have eaten your fill, and built fine houses to live in . . . beware lest your heart grow haughty . . . and you say to yourselves: "My own power and the strength of my own hand have won this wealth for me". Remember that it is . . . your God who gives you the power to get wealth . . .' (Deuteronomy 8:12–18). Would Egyptian bondage be replaced by slavery to the material world, to inquisitive impulses, to resurgent feelings of omnipotence?

Security

These questions still resonate today. Incarnated in these foundational texts is the disturbing, subversive call to develop a more dispassionate view of our material achieve-ments. For our natural self-centredness leads us to see material success as the result of our personal efforts alone. But it has never been true that energy and virtue are always rewarded. Nor have indolence and stupidity ever been a bar to the amassing of wealth.

Nowadays, more than ever, we recognise that a person's responsibility for their own financial well-being is not solely in their own hands. We might have come to believe that there is no problem big enough that decent marketing can't solve it, but as we lie awake in bed at night worrying about our work, our income, our pensions, our investments, we also know that we are dependent on forces far more powerful than ourselves. Preoccupied as we are with how much we earn, how much we spend, how much we save, we try to keep at bay the discomforting knowledge that in our global-ised economy we have little control over our financial security.

For beyond anxieties about money that may be rooted in our own psychological make-up, we are inextricably bound up with the capriciousness of markets. Our personal insecur-ities are interwoven with collective financial insecurities which can start off in one far-off part of the world and sweep across the planet like a speeded-up version of a medieval plague. The microchip-driven bacillus of economic in-stability can bring mighty nations to their knees. And it is a fantasy to think that we can remain immune to this disease.

The gods of finance can blow hot or cold and the limits of our own power are mercilessly exposed. 'Money', famously, 'can't buy me love.' Nor can it buy us security. Yet who is brave enough to deny that we still 'care too much for money' for our own peace of mind, our own spiritual well-being?

What are we to do? Can we develop spiritual perspectives towards money which acknowledge our human need for adequate material comfort; which recognise the limitations of our own efforts and strivings for security; which see that our mutual human interdependence may require from us more mindfulness about how our personal and societal finances are organised and disbursed?

Idealism and pragmatism

One radical approach in the past, adopted by monastic Christianity, was the move towards self-impoverishment. Not a goal in itself, but the means whereby a path is smoothed towards a higher goal: care for others. An imitation of the selfless love of Jesus leads to the adoption of 'poverty' – freedom from the acquisition of material goods – as a form of commitment to the needs of the world rather than one's own desires. An honourable solution to the dilemma of human acquisitiveness, but one which seemed to make more demands on the human soul than the majority of souls could bear.

Historically, Judaism tended to take a more pragmatic approach. Based on the biblical precedents, rabbinic leaders developed an elaborate framework for the regulation of financial and monetary matters. Business dealings were imbued with a practical ethical dimension. For example, once the price was agreed for the sale of property or goods to either a Jew or gentile, that price had to be honoured even if someone else offered more. It was even a religious duty, a spiritual discipline, to adhere to the 'thoughts in one's heart': 'if one has it in mind to sell something at a certain price, and the purchaser, not aware of it, offers more, one shall take only the amount at which one had decided to sell it, so that one may fulfil what is written [in the Psalms, 15:2]: "And speaks the truth in one's heart . . ." '

This kind of legislation was an attempt to nurture a spiritual stance towards – *a way of being with* – money. Money was not an end in itself but a medium through which honesty, integrity, goodness – the soul's outer garments – could be practised. Economic activity was both an expression of the soul and a form of soul-making.

Much emphasis too was placed on the avoidance of conspicuous consumption, and the practical redistribution of wealth. Ten per cent of a person's annual income had to be given to charity. And charity was not an amorphous concept. The most influential voice of rabbinic Judaism, Moses Maimonides (1135–1204), detailed eight degrees in the giving of *tzedakah*, starting with one who gives 'grudgingly, reluctantly or with regret' – this was still acceptable because who knows how the giving could transform the giver once the act was done, let alone help the recipient? – through 'giving before one is asked', to 'giving anonymously', and so on up to the highest level of giving: 'the act of someone who, through a gift, a loan, or by finding them employment, helps another to become self-supporting'.

The Hasidic master Nachman of Bratslav captured the essence of this strand of Judaic spirituality. He taught that how we use our money is a practical spiritual manifestation of 'loving one's neighbour' in which money is a form of energy, facilitating transformation of oneself and others. Similarly, in our own age, the New Age thinker Deepak Chopra, speaking out of a Hindu spiritual tradition, articulates this alternative perspective: 'The word affluence means "to flow in abundance". Money is really a symbol of the life energy . . .'

This is a radical vision. The challenge glitters and shimmers before us: combining inner attention and outer action, can we move from enslavement to money towards a way of being with money that has the liberating potential to spark the divine within our souls? From Victorian philanthropy to the neo-Buddhist philosophy of modern millionaire business executives, we see the attempt to reconcile God and Mammon: making money, spending money, donating money becomes part of a spiritual journey towards the re-sacralisation of everyday life.

Nothingness

Religions are beautiful because of the strong possibility that they are founded on nothing.

John Ashbery, poet, USA

When [the Kabbalist text] the *Zohar* speaks expressly of such a nothing, it is always taken as God's innermost mode of being . . . 'Nothing' is the first and highest of the *sefirot*.

Gershom Scholem, professor of Jewish mysticism

God made everything out of nothing. But the nothing shows through.

Paul Valéry, French poet

Nullity

We have reached the mid-point of the journey. The still, dark point of the turning world. We have long known we would have to face it: the heart of darkness coiled at the core of our being. We have been carrying it with us since the beginning, catching it momentarily out of the corner of our eye: the horror of being. The horror of the suffering enacted by nature and executed by humankind. The horror of the suffering endured through sickness and starvation, earthquake and floods, the targeted terrors and the casual daily cruelties. And the horror of our forthcoming absence from the life of the world: the shadow of death hovering behind us and beneath us and within us.

The twentieth century came to a close on 11 September 2001. The malevolent tentacles of humanity's long and barbaric civil war stretch from the trenches of the Somme to the twisted wreckage of the World Trade Center. From zero yards gained on the ground to Ground Zero. One hundred and eighty million killed: from the cannon-fodder of the First World War to industrialised genocide at Auschwitz to the melted flesh of Dresden and Hiroshima to the Soviet and Chinese gulags to the killing fields of Cambodia and Rwanda and Bosnia. The litany of horror is seared into our souls.

This anti-liturgy mocks our pretensions. The spirituality of everyday life? Rather than an alphabet of paradise, we could sketch out an alphabet of hell: an alternative world-view where our precious human potential, our fragile giftedness, is dwarfed by the monstrous, barbarous inventivenesss of our disposition towards evil. Where our inspiration and creativity and compassion are voided by disasters and diseases and deprivations, all the suffering to which humanity is heir. Where what we achieve crumbles to nothing, what we can aspire to collapses into nothingness. Entropy's final victory: the creation of nothing out of what is. The nullity of everyday life.

Yet nothingness as antithetical to life is not the whole story.

For nothingness is also the fullness of life.

Ayin

Nothingness lies on the underside of our experience, moment by moment. It is the space between our words, the silence beneath our speech, the white spaces between the black letters inscribed on the parchment of our lives. Nothingness reveals itself within everyday language and thought and activity – in the gaps, in the hesitancies, in the doubts and uncertainties – as if there is an alternative hidden 'text' to our lives, a shadow story haunting our being. It can feel too frightening to hear it, too daunting to pay attention to it. Yet impregnated into the body of life is the seed of nothingness. It fertilises in the dark. It may scare us; or intrigue us; or, on occasion, inspire us.

But nothing can save us from it.

For Nothing is its name.

Within the Kabbalistic tradition there was a recognition that God's limitless being could not be represented within the ordinary confines of human language. So some preferred to call divine being *Ayin*: 'Nothing'. 'Nothing' unfolded itself at all times and in all places, filling the crevices of life, the cracks between intentions and actions, between thoughts and speech, between language and silence. This nothingness flowed in us and through us and around us. And spiritual life came to be seen as learning to be attentive to, and participating in, this unfolding process of being with nothingness.

Being and nothingness shadowed each other, like life and death. 'God' was both being and nothingness – for 'God' was One. And if each human being was created in the 'image and likeness' of God (Genesis 1:26), it meant that we too consisted of both being and nothingness. Our task was to align them within ourselves, to gain a perspective on our lives so that we could fully participate in the manifold exuberance of being while recognising its limitations, its lack of definitiveness, its transience.

109

Creation was seen as God's wrestling of being out of nothingness so that there was enough space for humanity to mirror this creativity, to reflect the glory of the struggle. And this, despite the suffering conjoined to our souls, is what we do. The stories that are our lives – and the stories we generate through our creativity and inventiveness – reveal the triumph (and defiance) of the human spirit in the face of our forthcoming absence from the life of the world.

Stories

'After Auschwitz, it is no longer possible to write poetry . . .' declared the German social philosopher Theodor Adorno in 1949. He believed that when art tried to transfigure suffering it trivialised it, and did an injustice to its victims. Yet surrounded as we are by the forces of barbarism, of chaos, of nothingness, the powers of the human creative imagination seem to equip us for coexistence with the darkness of being. It is extraordinary to see how the human spirit blossoms out of the dungheap of human misery. There is an irrepressible urge in us to create, to procreate, to reaffirm the value of life in the face of the nullity of being. Over and again, out of the midst of nothing there is the reaffirmation of desire, the drive to overcome disaster, destruction, despair, to champion survival over defeatedness and the denial of being.

Later in life Adorno conceded that, in spite of his earlier pronouncement, 'it is now virtually in art alone that suffering can still find its own voice, consolation, without immediately being betrayed . . .' (1962). Primo Levi's writings are an example of this, magisterial explications by a Holocaust survivor of the possibility that the human spirit could keep at bay the forces of dehumanisation.

Levi gave each chapter of *The Periodic Table* (1975) the name of a chemical element. The chapters, allegorical yet autobiographically based, illuminate the elemental nature of human desires, the tensions between creativity and destructiveness, and the randomness surrounding matters of life and death. Midway through his book, Levi placed two pieces of fiction written during the war and inserted in his non-fictional narrative 'like a prisoner's dream of escape'.

We too might dream of escaping the prison of everyday life, and the terrors the world endures. But which is an illusion: the prison or the dream of escape?

The narrative that follows takes as its point of departure a biblical story. The book of Genesis introduces us to Abraham, the putative founder of a new religious consciousness which intuited that a single elemental energy underlies all of life. The name given to that life energy, the being of the universe, was *Adonai*: 'that which was, is, will be'; 'the One who Is'; 'Being' – who later became recognised as 'Nothing'. The future of this new mode of perception lay with Abraham's heirs, and in particular his son Isaac. And yet a father's murderous impulses almost sabotage the destiny of the whole project.

Genesis 22 tells of the binding of Isaac (the *Akedah)* when Abraham, impelled by a force he believed to be divine, took his beloved son on a journey into the unknown, three days distant, with wood and fire, until he reached a place where he was ready to sacrifice his son, his future, his destiny. Life and death, separated only by the blade of a knife. And a holocaust – that is, 'a burnt sacrificial offering' – avoided only by the intervention of a different understanding of the divine. A voice which chooses life over death, which tests the limits of our humanity by showing us that destructiveness and hopefulness, being and nothingness, are fused within us – not to say confused. We are made up of both. Can we learn to refine our sensitivities to their coexistence within us so that our futures are not squandered, our hopes crushed, our dreams extinguished in the fire of our elemental passions?

Like the best literature, the text challenges us to look again at our certainties, to consider what we believe, to examine the gaps between the words of our mouths and the meditations of our hearts. Genesis 22 does not mention Sarah, Abraham's wife and the mother of Isaac. After these things, she never appears again. Her story is untold. As if her story is nothing.

Sarah's story

Three days I waited, then three days more: restless, anxious, a woman waiting for her husband and son to return. I was the beginning of that long, devoted chain of self-denying enchained women. The ones who always waited for their men to return – from war, from sports (frivolous or deadly), from other women, from all the machismo and magnificence and madness that men find it in their nature to pursue. And we wait to hear about all the sacrifices they have made – for us, for the family, for the sake of the future.

But from now on there will be no more waiting. For those six days, six nights, I, Sarah, was that wife and mother who waited, who searched the horizon for a sign that my menfolk were safe, had returned from testing their manhood, their endurance, their faith, or whatever other pathetic justification they would give for their journey, their absence. All that rhetoric – of initiation, of the necessary sacrifices – but for me there was just three days there and three days back, tracing them in my mind, no rest.

Then just before night fell, with that swift, sharp, cold suddenness of the desert, as the sun sliced like a knife into the horizon, blood red, the life draining out of the day – I saw them. First the lads, then the animals, a knot of figures, dust, obscuring vision. Then in the gloaming, there, it was him: Avraham, Avraham avinu, father of the tribe, my husband – but wedded more to his own unyielding certainties than to me. Still it was him, framed against the darkling sky. I laughed. Again. Relief and bitterness.

But now, eyes straining against the deepening gloom, where was he, my only one, my precious? Where is he? Hidden by the dust? Dust to dust. Where is Isaac?

I had the dream on the third night. I saw my son, but it was not my son. His upturned face was demonic, though his voice was the voice I knew.

'What has your father done to you?'

'He took me and led me up, far away from here. It was high up. He built up an altar, arranged the wood upon it, bound me up, took up the knife, he was going to cut me up, I looked up at his face, I saw that faraway look, rapture, like listening to a supplication from on high . . . "No, don't – don't do it" . . . Without that look, that voice, that rupture, I would have been slaughtered on the spot.'

I began to cry, in the dream, to sob, to wail, like the sound of the shofar, the call of death. And with it I woke myself up.

And the tears were real. But for whom was I crying?

When I had been told that I was to give birth, I laughed. After so long, after all hope had dissolved, I would have a child, a future. Continuity. Such joy at the possibility. Such joy at the enlargement of my horizon. Such a bearable lightness of being after all that diminution of hope, the slow contraction into despair. The joy in that laughter. And the scepticism. Who could believe this?

I had been so harsh, in my sadness. And jealous. When Hagar conceived, in my place, I could not bear to look. I sent her away, with the child in her womb. I sent her into the desert, to die, that I could live nursing my own sadness and regret for all that could not be, for all that I had failed to give birth to in my own life. But she returned, gave birth, and even though I had my own child later – a miracle, they said – I could never forgive her for having taken my place. I could never forgive the fact that what I had wanted to repress had returned: that Egyptian with eyes only for him, and her son Ishmael with eyes that looked daggers at my beloved one, my Isaac.

Or was it my eyes that looked daggers, when I saw them play together, laugh together, wrestle together in the dust? Dust to dust. I sent them both away, a second time. Hatred in my heart. They were to be a sacrifice – for my own peace of mind. Cast out of sight what we cannot bear to see. When the envy or the jealousy or the rivalry get too much, when the bitterness can no longer be contained, kill off what we cannot face. They were my sacrifice, Hagar and Ishmael, my Akedah. *My hand on the knife.*

When I awoke, crying, they were tears of remorse, tears of regret, tears of fear. The horror at one's heart of darkness. Not just Abraham. Me too. All of us. Murdering the future, knowingly, unknowingly. Destroying hopes, killing off potential, cancelling out the very possibility of transformation, that things could be different.

And when they returned, back from beyond the horizon, I knew that there would be no more waiting, no more prevarication. No more waiting for someone else to take responsibility for my life. Isaac was there, of course. He'd been obscured, in my sight, by his father. But all I could see were his ashes, what could have been, the holocaust that would have ended my story. When I saw him, a survivor, I felt the unbearable lightness of being. I saw that his survival changed nothing. His return did not erase my awareness of what might have been. In the dark Sabbath night, after the week of waiting, worrying, dreaming, I saw in a moment of stillness, of perfect rest, that there is but a hair's-breadth that separates life from death.

Like falling indelibly into the past, I saw myself high up, on that mountain, knife in hand and bound to the altar, suffering the vertigo of existence. I saw the nothingness that lies coiled in the very core of being, like a worm. The contingency of life. The knife's edge that separates us from the abyss. And at that moment I felt myself die, diving into the vortex of nothingness without which knowledge all hope is forlorn, all certainties are an illusion. I saw that nothingness was the very eye of God. The eye which stares, unblinking, unconcerned. I am what I am. The Holy nothingness of being. I, Sarah, princess of life, wife of Abraham, mother of Isaac, mother of the tribe, unguarded, unprepared, exposed to thoughts that do often lie too deep for tears.

I shiver in the darkness. I look up at the stars, glimmering like memories, intimating our future. The stars are indispensable, the vast brain of time, a galaxy of fire set by no human hand. The universe in which there are no utopias and no betrayals, neither faith nor its absence. No mothers, no fathers, no children, no justice, or injustice. The inconceivable spectacle of no antagonism. Too late in life, a new beginning flickers into view: annihilation is certain and therefore all human endeavour is futile; annihilation is certain and therefore all human endeavour is victorious. The waiting is over. Something like a smell of incense hovers in the cold night air.

Orifices

---

orifice n: the entrance or outlet of any body cavity ... an opening through which something may pass ...

Longman Dictionary of the English Language

If we picture the mind as an orifice then we cannot help but wonder what it should be open to and what it should be open for.

Adam Phillips, psychoanalyst

Ways in

'So what's "O" going to be?' friends asked when I said I was writing an A–Z of spirituality. 'Openness? ... Open-mindedness? ... Order? ... Observances?' They were plausible possibilities – and I'll touch on all of them in this chapter. But 'Orifices'? How's that connected to spirituality? A good question. But good questions can be spiritual acts: they help us to remain open to new thoughts, new insights, to inspiration and wonder, to the pleasurable challenge of living with minds making space for what is not yet known,

116

rather than with our minds already made up, and thus closed to life and the fluidity and strangeness of being.

Mouth, nose, vagina, urethra, anus – these are the five major bodily orifices. If we direct our attention to each of them we can appreciate how our sense of well-being in the world is intimately dependent on how well they function. Breathing, eating, excreting, sexual pleasure, childbirth and human survival – these are all at stake as we reflect on the role of our bodily orifices. Suffering, illness, perhaps even death await, once an orifice fails us. They have natural, physiological jobs to do; and we use them, misuse them, or simply take them for granted – up until the moment when they let us down. Orifices can discomfort us on a daily basis: bad breath, toothache, ulcers and sores, farts, constipation, sexual secretions, urinary infections, thrush, diarrhoea . . . all those conspicuous or secret conditions that unnerve us and sometimes blight our lives. Frightening, the distress our humanity causes us.

Our own orifices are the sites of both pleasure and pain. And other people's orifices too. They fascinate and attract us, repel us, generate endless fantasies in us. Orifices make people seem permeable. They are the passageways to the inside, to the hidden, to the not-yet-revealed. We want to be close to someone, to 'enter into' their world. Their body is a conduit, penetrable somehow or another in ways we think their minds may not be. Our curiosity about what goes on inside another person focuses, sometimes consciously but often unconsciously, on their orifices. We imagine our way in. We want to know what's going on inside, we want to overcome our separateness, we want to put ourselves inside them, we want them inside of us.

The spiritual longing for union is often enacted within our interpersonal relationships. The orgasm has replaced the eucharist, the cross, the Torah, as a focus of longing and an image of fulfilment. Lovers feed each other, couples explore each other's body cavities, a partner's openings may invite

117

our desire to submit to a power whose intensity may take us by surprise (a desire once called worship), possessing us to possess the other. Losing ourselves in order to find ourselves, as of old. Through the bodily orifices a hallowed drama is played out: the exhilaration of contact with another, overcoming one's separation, the flowing sensuousness of life, the yearning for completeness, merging into the unity of being. Desire's consummation.

Fragility

Jewish tradition has long recognised that the efficient functioning of our bodies is integral to our sense of well-being. Morning services start with a prayer-meditation, a 'blessing of thanksgiving' which acknowledges that we human beings are, before anything else, creatures of flesh and blood:

> You are blessed, Eternal our God, the energy within existence, who forms humanity in wisdom, creating in us orifices and passageways. It is transparently known . . . that if any one of them were opened or any one of them were closed [when they shouldn't be], it would be impossible to exist, or to stand in your presence. Blessed are you, the eternal energy which heals all flesh and acts wondrously.

This 1500–year-old reflection on the wondrous, fragile nature of our bodily well-being is not a detached, objective statement. It's a poignant acknowledgement that our breathing, digestion, metabolism and evacuation of waste matter have a 'wisdom' of their own on which we are daily dependent. And gratitude is the order of the day.

Traditional Jews also recite this blessing after going to the toilet. Spirituality is not divorced from the most mundane of our activities: pissing and shitting are to be treated with reverence. Whenever we encounter problems with either we glimpse the truthfulness of the sentiment that if things go seriously wrong with the opening and closing of our orifices 'it would be impossible to exist'. This meditation inculcates in us a humble recognition of our essential fragility. It is an antidote to our omnipotence and our casual acceptance that good health is some kind of 'right' that life owes to us.

Sex

As we saw previously (cf. 'Food'), Jewish religious culture found ways to help the individual develop attentiveness towards the sublime diversity of being. Blessings were moments of attunement to the unfolding majesty and quirkiness of life on earth. They deepened one's experience of being alive and instilled an awareness of one's dependence on an animating energy other than ourselves. They were opportunities for spiritual enrichment. Whether it was tasting food, encountering elements of the natural world, or recognising the awesome quiddity of a host of daily sense-experiences, such moments of silent or spoken blessing could revivify one's easily jaded appreciation for what is and what can be. Yet strangely, Judaism never developed a blessing for sex: neither before sex, nor after sex.

Why not? Does this indicate a repressive attitude towards human sexuality? Are faeces OK but not semen? Is our ability to urinate more a cause for wonder than the sweat and saliva and juices which can manifest themselves when two human beings come together? There were some rabbinic thinkers who did consider the male and female sexual drive to be so problematic for human relationships and so destructive, potentially, of the social order that it were best if sex was thought of as a somewhat burdensome responsibility, to be performed only for the purposes of fulfilling the religious duty of procreation.

Perhaps too they felt, like Aristotle, that sexual pleasure undermines our rationality; and thus is a threat to the mental discipline needed to order a just society. And further, that the polymorphous emotional unboundedness of sexual

119

desire is a threat to the self-discipline needed for spiritual growth. This nexus of anxieties within ancient Judaic culture – anxieties shared by many religious traditions – may underlie the fact that sex was denied its own sanctifying blessing.

But this quasi-ascetic tradition was not the only rabbinic view. Sexuality was also seen more congenially as an aspect of God's beneficent creation, with sexual activity both a natural part of human self-expressiveness and an opportunity for spiritual experience. The medieval rabbinic legislator and mystic Nahmanides (1194–1270) describes this stance: sexuality as created by God and as a means of exploring how divine energy manifests itself within the human realm.

> Know that the sexual intercourse of man and woman is holy and pure . . . We the possessors of the Holy Torah believe that God . . . created all, as His wisdom decreed, and did not create anything ugly or shameful . . . He created man and woman. He created and formed all their organs and orifices, placed them in their form. And he did not create anything repulsive . . . Know that the male is the mystery of wisdom and the female is the mystery of understanding. And the pure sex act is the mystery of knowledge . . . If so, it follows that proper sexual union can be a means of spiritual elevation . . .

Although this benign approach to sexuality pertained in that era only to married couples, it reflected an evolving rabbinic precept that whatever gave sexual pleasure to both parties (oral and anal sex included) was permitted. Through our orifices we could celebrate the life of divine being reflected within our human being.

So why no blessing before or after sex? Already by the Middle Ages Judaic blessings had the sacred carapace of ancient rabbinic authority encrusted around them. Innovation was viewed with suspicion. This over-reverence for the pre-existing formalised authority of the past haunts Jewish religious and spiritual practice, as it perhaps haunts all Western religious traditions. So the absence of a blessing for sex is a gap in traditional Judaic consciousness.

Nowadays, however, anyone seeking to enhance their spiritual practice can create their own. We can bless that eternal energy within existence which ripples through our bodies, allowing us to find closeness with others: through difference we find likeness, through knowing another we come to know ourselves, physical and spiritual beings reflecting the image of the divine. We bless that eternal energy which teaches that all real living is meeting.

We take our cue from the inclusion in the biblical canon of the erotically charged duet that is the Song of Songs:

> Like an apple tree among trees of the forest,
> So is my beloved among the youths.
> I delight to sit in his shade
> And his fruit is sweet to my mouth . . .
> His banner of love was over me

2:3–4

> Sweetness drops from your lips, O bride
> Honey and milk are under your tongue . . .
> A garden locked
> Is my own, my bride,
> a fountain locked, a sealed-up spring . . .

4:11–12

The sexual symbolism of the book – the imagery of orifices available and sought after – was seen as an integral part of holy literature. Rabbi Akiva deployed a daring metaphor (the inner sanctum of the Temple) to describe the relationship between this love poem and the other sacred narratives of the canon. All of scripture was holy, he said, 'but the Song of Songs is the holy of holies'. He read its sensual lyricism as portraying the relationship of mutual desire and longing between God and the community of Israel: a passionate engagement between a divine lover and an enthralled

121

people. (A people who throughout their history have sought to reciprocate that love: within the Jewish mystical tradition the highest form of prayer was described as 'intercourse with the Presence'.)

And just as God's love caressed souls and penetrated hearts and minds, human sensuality was the earthly counterpart of this spiritual drama. Opening one's body and mind to the presence of another was standing in the presence of that animating energy of being called *Adonai*: the One who was, is, will be.

Listening in

The lack of a blessing for human sexual activity betrays the ancient Judaic ambivalence about orifices. And there's a similar gap in relation to menstruation. The biblical-rabbinic tradition prohibited sex during the menstrual period, and for a week afterwards. Although this practice is still adhered to by many traditionally observant Jews, the majority of modern-minded Jews have long since rejected this concept of 'uncleanness' as demeaning and archaic.

Yet paradoxically it has been a new generation of contemporary Jewish feminist thinkers who have pointed to the potential within this apparently regressive tradition. Could it be developed into a spiritual practice which honours the remarkable nature of the female body's capacity to both generate and cast off a potential new life? Could it be adapted to become part of a rhythm of separation and renewed closeness between sexual partners, a way of nurturing excitement and desire? Could new blessings be developed for when one's period begins and ends each month? For a girl's first period – the transition into womanhood? For the ending of menstruation in one's middle years? Moments in life when orifices reveal the mystery of being.

God's dominant (and dominating) orifice – his mouth – no longer speaks. No transcendent voice issues from on high

to tell us how to live our lives, how to honour our physicality, how to retain our sense of the sacredness of our bodily
orifices in daily life. What we have, though, are our own
minds, that mysterious orifice with which we can listen to,
and celebrate, what is revealed within us: 'I have ceased
to listen to stars and books. I have begun to listen to the
teachings my blood whispers to me' (Herman Hesse).

Pleasure

On the Day of Judgement, a person will have to give account for every good thing they might have enjoyed and did not.

Talmud

Pleasure and selfhood

This chapter was going to be about Prayer: it seemed the obvious theme to explore within an A–Z of spirituality. But there are plenty of manuals on prayer and the spirituality of prayer, far fewer on the spirituality of pleasure. At first glance one can see why. Prayer, after all, is at the heart of Western religious teaching and practice, while pleasure has frequently received a bad press from religion, which seems to offer a stark choice between selflessness and selfishness, between pleasing God and pleasing yourself. As if pleasure is too threatening to the dedication, devotion and sense of duty traditionally associated with following a religious path. As if pleasure inevitably subverts our sense of responsibility, undermines our capacity for concern, is antithetical to self-sacrifice or moral wisdom.

But why does a commitment to the spirituality of everyday

life preclude taking pleasure in what life holds and offers? Why is it that we think there's a dichotomy between spiritual exploration and personal pleasure?

There is a story told about Rabbi Zusya of Hanipol, who one day failed to arrive as usual at the study-house. His students went to his home, where they found him ill in bed, trembling, with blankets pulled over his shoulders.

'I am dying,' he said, 'and I'm very frightened.'

'Why are you afraid?' asked his favourite student. 'Surely you of all people can't be worried that God will find fault with you? All your life you kept the commandments as faithfully as Moses. All your life you prayed as steadily as Abraham. Why then should you fear to face God?'

'You don't understand,' replied Zusya, 'for if God asks me why I didn't act like Moses, I can tell him I was not Moses. If God asks me why I didn't behave like Abraham, I can tell him I wasn't Abraham. But when God says "Zusya, how can you account for those times when you failed to be Zusya?" – what can I tell him then?'

What I appreciate about this Hasidic story, simple though it is, is its down-to-earth (but radical) approach to religiosity. It doesn't denigrate either prayer or obedience to traditional moral, ethical or ritual norms. But it does suggest that conformity to externally dictated behaviour is not a substitute for that more elusive spiritual imperative: living from (and living up to) the full potential of our selfhood. Of course to live in this way we have to pay attention to who, and what, that 'self' might be.

The pleasure of being human

We start off in life as *innately pleasure-seeking* beings. In our earliest months and years our instinctual pleasure-seeking desires – for the sensual warmth of loving hands, for nurture and security and stimulation, for a safely-bounded-yet-exciting exploration of the world around us – are integral to our growing sense of self. But, for a variety of reasons, this natural quest for pleasure is not always welcomed or valued or even recognised by those whose task it is to care for us. Our pleasure-seeking selves become disturbed, distorted, or perhaps the source of shame.

If aspects of our early self-expressiveness are squashed or ignored or condemned, pleasure in adult life, though longed for and sought after, proves ephemeral and insubstantial. That fullness of self we yearn for – the source of our spiritual depth – remains elusive. Struggle as we might to 'be ourselves', to feel pleasurably alive, we remain unfulfilled, gnawed by an inner emptiness.

But how are we to experience a fullness of being, and take pleasure in being ourselves, when 'being ourselves' has become a self-serving cliché, a mantra to justify self-indulgence? Pleasure-seeking, with its attendant emotional uninhibitedness, sometimes seems a symptom of the shallow soullessness of our age. Without a diligent, discriminating intelligence helping to discern what our souls need, the pursuit of personal pleasure can be destructive of our spiritual potential.

One of the greatest modern chroniclers of our spiritual bewilderment is the novelist Saul Bellow. Here he is, in *Mr. Sammler's Planet* (1970), with the ardour of a biblical prophet, casting his dispassionate yet compassionate Judaic gaze on our contemporary state of being:

> It has only been in the last two centuries that the majority of people in civilised countries have claimed the privilege of being individuals. Formerly they were slave, peasant, labourer, even artisan, but not person. It is clear that this revolution, a triumph for justice in many ways . . . has also introduced new kinds of grief and misery, and so far, on the broadest scale, it has not been altogether a success . . . For a historian, of great interest, but for one aware of the suffering it is appalling.

Hearts that get no real wage, souls that find no nourishment. Falsehoods, unlimited. Desire, unlimited. Possibility, unlimited ... The idea of the uniqueness of the soul. An excellent idea. A true idea. But in these forms? In these poor forms. Dear God! With hair, with clothes, with drugs and cosmetics, with genitalia, with trips through evil, monstrosity, and orgy, with even God approached through obscenities? How terrified the soul must be in this vehemence.

So we find ourselves – and have to 'find' and 'be' ourselves – in what Bellow elsewhere describes as a 'moronic inferno'. In that chaotic state in which we live now, where we can feel overwhelmed by all kinds of outer forces – political, economic, cultural, technological, military – which carry everything before them with a kind of disorder in which we are supposed to survive with all our human qualities intact. Who really has sufficient internal cohesiveness to resist, to flourish, to 'be themselves'? Pleasure, so-called, is drip-fed to us within a 24/7 culture of relentlessly trivialised infotainment. But if we only consume junk pleasures we shouldn't wonder that our souls remain hungry. It's no wonder that pleasure has so often been seen as antithetical to spiritual development.

And yet our capacity to appreciate, and take pleasure in, what surrounds us – and what we can make from what surrounds us – is a defining characteristic of our humanity. Within personal relationships, in our relationship to the natural world and to the arts, at work and as we relax, opportunities for pleasure open up and enable us to experience a sense of well-being. Not the frantically sought-after 'pleasures' that Bellow chronicles, which delight in their own superficiality, but the pleasures of being more fully human: when we sense our connectedness to the unfolding being implanted within existence, nearer to us than we dare to believe. Pleasures that caress and nurture the soul, rather than impoverish or terrify it. *And we do know the difference.*

Genuine pleasure enhances our sense of well-being, lifts and expresses our spirits, ennobles us so that we can feel a grateful and humble satisfaction in being alive, being human, being ourselves. So what stands in the way of this kind of pleasure?

Perfection

One of the major stumbling-blocks to the soul's capacity to experience pleasure is the unconscious wish for perfection ingrained within us. Just as we seek the perfect partner, relationship, job, holiday, we also seek the spiritual equivalent: some perfect state of being, when we will be enlightened or whole or calm or selfless or wise (or all of them together).

But perfection is the bane of spiritual endeavour. The evangelist Matthew's exhortation echoes through Western culture: 'Be perfect, as your father in heaven is perfect' (5:48). What are we to make of this? The New Testament text uses the Greek *teleos*, which means 'complete' or 'finished' – and by extension 'perfect'. This imports the Greek longing for perfection into the Hebraic world view – where *holiness* rather than perfection was the aim of human striving.

Perfection can be accomplished, though, only by the elimination of everything inadequate – an impossible and omnipotent fantasy. Whereas holiness involves an acceptance of limitations, divine and human. *Holiness is movement towards.* It is active, dynamic, always evolving, a creative process of being and becoming. Whereas the quest for perfection involves destruction. It can never be satisfied with what is, it can never take pleasure in the not-yet-finished, the quotidian, the stuff of daily life. There can be no contentment, for everything must be surpassed, surmounted, en route to the final destination. The goal? A state of stasis – which is antithetical to the unfolding rhythm of life, to being's fluidity. Perfection: the terrorising final solution to life's vitalising incompleteness.

In the Hebrew Bible God is never described as 'perfect'. Although the divine has human qualities attributed to it we don't find perfection amongst them. The nearest Hebrew term to 'perfect', *tamim*, is used of animals, who must be 'healthy' or 'without blemish' if offered for sacrifice. *Tamim* is also used in parallel with words like truth and justice to describe a human activity done with 'integrity'. And occasionally *tamim* is used to describe people.

Noah, for example, is described as 'a just man and perfect in his generation' (Genesis 6:9). But the King James' translation here is dependent on pre-existing notions of perfection within Western Christian consciousness. The Hebrew text reads: Noah 'was a righteous man, completely so (*tamim*) in relation to his generation'. So *tamim* qualifies the quality of being 'righteous'. The narrator is suggesting that Noah was as righteous as it was possible to be *within the context in which he found himself*, 'in his generation'. This moral relativism is unsettling if one looks to the Bible for absolutes. It disturbs, as the Hebrew Bible so often seems to do, our wish for perfect heroes. Noah's righteousness didn't stop him getting drunk after the flood and being sodomised by his son (Genesis 9:21–2).

And what of Abraham, father of nations? The text presents us with the divine instruction: 'Walk before me and be thou perfect' (Genesis 17:1). Again, the Authorised Version fails to do justice to the nuances of the Hebrew, which reads 'Walk before me and *be* ... completely (*tamim*)'. The emphasis is on the verb: on *being*. On trying to *be* with the fullness of one's humanity.

As Zusya realised, biblical characters aren't idealised models to be copied. They are flawed human beings, struggling with what it means to be human. The goal isn't perfection, but a diligent attentiveness to the never-completed task of expressing one's complex humanity with as much integrity as one can muster. This is spirituality for everyday life. Wrestling with the pain and the pleasure of being human.

Coming home

Taking pleasure in the simple day-to-day realities that surround us is a spiritual discipline. The secret seems to lie not so much in 'doing' but in 'being'. Being with what is present – and what is presented. The pleasure of an unexpected phone-call, a family celebration, looking at old photos, listening to music, playing with a pet, being engrossed in a novel, glimpsing the sunset between the houses, hearing the night owl, helping someone in need, singing, dancing, praying in a community, gardening, unwrapping a present, the intimacy of sex, writing in one's diary, doing a piece of work with attention to what occurs at each moment, studying a devotional text, speaking in depth to another person . . .

It's not the activities in themselves which necessarily give us pleasure, but how we are with them. Or how they are with us. For pleasure is a gift. We can't force pleasure to happen. We can only play our part in being open to what is presented to us. We can develop our sensitivity to the spiritual even if we can never create it on demand. Pleasure: a kind of homecoming.

> Sunlight, passing through banyan trees, throws patterns on the opposite side of the room. It is late afternoon. Indian crows land on the window sill. Their elongated shadows stalk across the floor. The moment opens out and I am in a flow of present-ness, cleaved from the past and not straining for the future. I am in the only true home we can ever have: this, here, now.
> *Robyn Davidson, author and traveller*

Quiet

It is not necessary that you leave the house. Remain at your table and listen. Do not even listen, simply wait. Do not even wait, be wholly still and alone. The world will present itself to you for its unmasking: it has no choice, in ecstasy it will writhe at your feet.

Franz Kafka

Be still – and know that I am God

Psalm 46:10

Distractions

Silence is frightening. It throws us back on ourselves. It presents us with our solitariness, our aloneness. We fear that aloneness, confusing it with loneliness. We surround ourselves with distractions: on our own at home, we turn on the TV; companionless car journeys are filled with CDs or the radio; when we relax on the beach or walk in the countryside, our mobile phone keeps us company. We must never be alone. We hum to ourselves as we work, we talk to ourselves in the dark. We must never be left with only the thoughts in our head. What would be unmasked if we stayed with the world inside us? It's too frightening to contemplate: the infinite space within.

Public spaces too have succumbed to our fears: we suffer muzak in lifts, hotels and bars, cinemas and stations, while we sit in restaurants or wait on the phone. Silence may be golden, but it's been tarnished long ago. Is it the chatter in our heads we fear, the cacophony of voices competing for attention, the sad or vicious conversations that go round and round, the endless background clatter, our wishes and hopes and dreads and desires: the inner tumult, the discordant ferment of our minds? Do we distract ourselves because we fear the babble and clamour within – or because we fear its absence? Is it our maddening inner disquiet we cannot bear – or do we fear what we'd find if it should stop? Without company, without diversions, in the quiet of our lives, what might we discover? What emptiness might silence uncover, what hollowness of being?

Or – more frightening still – what fullness of being might silence reveal, what writhing presence might show its face? 'If we had a keen vision and feeling of all ordinary human life, it would be like hearing the grass grow and the squirrel's heart beat, and we should die of that roar which lies on the other side of silence' (George Eliot, *Middlemarch*). So maybe it's death that scares us? Which silence, in some half known-about way, may seem to prefigure: 'No-one gets up after death – there is no applause – there is only silence and some second-hand clothes . . .' (Tom Stoppard, *Rosencrantz and Guildenstern are Dead*).

So is it God's absence that we fear? Must we block out the tinnitus of our solitary existence echoing in an indifferent universe? Or is it God's presence we fear? Hearing the still, small voice within the silence, whispering the secret meaning of our lives? No wonder we are terrified of silence. Yet also long for it. R. S. Thomas (1913–2000), Welsh poet and priest, writing against the grain of faith, speaks of

God:

>that great absence
In our lives, the empty silence
Within

We need quiet to hear that voice. The resonance of being.

A still, small voice

There are few axioms in this book in regard to spiritual practice. But here I want to risk one. *There can be no spiritual growth without silence.* Although we have come to depend on external stimulation to keep us going, our souls need respite from the ceaseless clamour of the world. Absence of silence stifles our spiritual growth: without the space to be quietly attentive to what is going on inside us, our capacity for reflective spiritual being is stunted. The rush of life drowns out the still, small voice within.

But what is this 'still, small voice'? The phrase comes from the biblical narrative concerning one of Israel's early prophets, Elijah, who arrives unannounced, without a genealogy or a history, in front of the idolatrous King Ahab, filled with an utter self-belief in his view of the world. There is no more dramatic entry in the Hebrew Bible. Angry, self-justifying, self-pitying, Elijah is a man consumed by the absolute certainty that he is right and that he, and only he, knows what God wants. In other words he's a fanatic. Yet beneath Elijah's manipulative and demanding behaviour, his aggression and zeal on behalf of a God with whom he so closely identifies, the narrator shows us a sad, lonely and insecure human being whose tragedy resides in his inability to face himself and his own destructive self-righteousness.

The climax of the mythic tale is beautifully told. Having slaughtered many hundreds of rival prophets at Mount Carmel after a theatrical demonstration of the power of Israel's God, Elijah flees the murderous vengeance of Ahab's wife, Jezebel. In the desert he becomes suicidal, but recovers enough composure to make the journey south to Horeb, the site of divine revelation. There he waits in a cave, and in the silence hears the voice of divine being asking: 'What is [there] for you here, Elijah?' (1 Kings 19:9).

This unsettling question – 'Why are you here? What are you doing here?' – is the one any of us might have to face were we to allow silence into our lives, and allow the silence to speak. But this inquiry is what we fear. As does Elijah. He launches into a passionate declaration of his faithfulness to his understanding of the divine; the destruction he has wrought on God's behalf; and his lonely fearfulness for his life. The response to this self-dramatisation is a symbolic moral admonition.

The text describes a mighty wind which shatters mountains and rocks, 'but the Eternal is not in the wind'. Then an earthquake, 'but the Eternal is not in the earthquake'. Then a fire, 'but the Eternal is not in the fire; but after the fire, *kol d'mamma dakka*: a still, small voice'. 'A small voice of silence'. 'A soundless stillness'. The precise meaning of the Hebrew is unclear. And that is right. The enigma of the divine presence within a voice of silence, within an absence of movement which contrasts so starkly with the noise and chaos and destructive energy that precedes it, is an enigma which evokes the mystery of being. Through silence we hear the eternal.

Poor Elijah, though, is lost. The same question as before is voiced: 'What is [there] for you here, Elijah?' (19:13). An opportunity for self-reflection presents itself. What has been learnt, understood, glimpsed in the demonstration of being which has just occurred? Nothing. Elijah repeats, word for unvarying word, his previous self-righteous, self-pitying lament–complaint (19:10, 14). Not the slightest insight has been gained. His furious, destructive nature (symbolised in the natural forces of wind, earthquake and fire) remains intransigent. Unaffected by the testimony of the 'still, small voice', he is dismissed by the narrative.

We are left with the irony of a prophet unmoved by a revelation of being, but whose refusal of mindfulness illuminates for us a fragment of the mystery in which we are enwrapped: that it is through stillness, through silence, through attending to the voice that speaks in the soundless space around us and within us, that we can come close to the meaning of being, and the meaning of our lives.

Being quiet

How can we learn to hear this 'still, small voice'? Or at least – because there are no guarantees – how do we create the most advantageous conditions whereby something of this small voice of silence might become available, accessible, audible beneath the hubbub of our lives? How do we find the quiet we need?

Here is one suggestion. *Set aside ten minutes a day to sit quietly on your own.* This is much harder than it sounds. Do it without distractions: no food, drink, chewing-gum, phones, reading material, music, TV. Nothing in your hands, your mouth, nothing to distract your five senses. Just sit. And be. Whatever thoughts, feelings, and bodily sensations arise in you, let them be there. Don't be afraid. You are being held. Gradually, day by day, something will happen. You will begin to observe your thoughts, feelings and bodily states, not just be pulled along by them. You can begin to watch them float by, like clouds.

You may have a favourite room to practise this exercise in being. Or a special chair. Or a cosy space on the floor, or on a bed. You are allowed to be comfortable. Some people find that lighting a candle helps them focus. You may want something to alert you when the time is up, so you don't get distracted by it. But don't get too busy. This is about 'being' not 'doing'. This is about slowing down, stopping, being with one's self. Ten minutes a day of quiet, to begin to hear the silence. Don't give up: something will happen. While waiting for the stillness you may feel fidgety, ridiculous, anxious, irritable or embarrassed – but don't give up. The still, small voice of silence, the soundless stillness, is waiting. It is there, here, present. It is presence.

You are learning to be still, to hear the silence within. You are learning to pay attention to the being of life beneath (and within) the doing of life. Wait. Wait without hope, for hope would be hope for the wrong thing. Wait and see. Wait and listen. Wait and observe. Wait until there is no waiting left. Just you, being, present. You are in the presence. You are the presence.

Other ways

You might find ten minutes a day too limiting. So give yourself twenty minutes. But better to start modestly than not to start at all. To find just ten minutes a day in lives so full of busyness is already pushing against our enslavement to activity. Those who do already have a regular meditative discipline will recognise this. But such periods of temporary withdrawal are vital to our well-being. The Hasidic leader Nachman of Bratslav considered such solitary being-with-one's-self the highest form of prayerfulness: 'Fix a time to go off by yourself to some room or field and express your thoughts and feelings to God in your own words. Pour out your whole heart . . . including your regrets . . .'

In contrast to ten minutes of quiet designed to find a way *underneath words* and into the silence, Nachman's time-honoured way is different. It asks us to gather together all our thoughts and feelings and offer them up *in words*. Yet nowadays someone following his guidance would be treated with suspicion. Such reclusivity can cause alarm in a homogenised culture of spurious bonhomie and superficial inclusivity.

But inclusivity too can play its part in developing one's attentiveness to the 'still, small voice'. It is possible to seek out like-minded souls in order to explore one's spirituality in a group. Groups dedicated to exploring inner work are not hard to find. Most religious traditions have such groups affiliated to them – though they tend to be seen as marginal – while other groups may follow the practices of non-denominational spiritual teachers such as Gurdjieff or Krishnamurti.

I have run exploratory spirituality groups for a number of years in a synagogue setting. Meeting regularly with a committed group of participants, we start with our personal life issues and spiritual concerns, followed by a period of silence – 'being with' ourselves, with each other, and with the space between us – followed by some time connecting our personal spiritual journeys with some textual material from the Judaic tradition, the wisdom of the past.

Over time, the silent reflectiveness at the heart of the evening infiltrates into the other time together. The attentiveness to what is going on, explored in the 'silent' time, carries into our conversations. One can be with one's inner silence even as one speaks, whether in a group or in everyday life. If the emphasis is on 'being' rather than 'doing' it is quite surprising what can happen. Learning to be still and listen is an art that can take years to achieve. Or it can happen in the twinkling of an eye.

Relationships

All real living is meeting.

Martin Buber

Talking turkey

There is a story, told by Nachman of Bratslav, about a prince who became mad and imagined he was a turkey. The prince took off his clothes, sat under the royal table and refused to eat anything except oats and crumbs. His father, the king, brought all the doctors of the land to him, but none could cure his son. At last a wise man came and undertook to cure the prince. Immediately the wise man took off his clothes and sat naked under the royal table next to the prince, and then began to scratch among the oats and crumbs.

The prince watched for a while, then asked: 'Who are you?'
Silence.

Then: 'What are you doing here?'
More silence.

Eventually the wise man asked: 'And who are you and what are you doing here?'

'I am a turkey,' said the prince.

'And I am a turkey too,' replied the wise man.

So the two turkeys sat there together till they grew accustomed to one another.

One day the wise man asked the king to hand him a vest. He put it on and, shocked, the prince said: 'What do you think you're doing?'

'Do you imagine that a turkey is not allowed to wear a vest?' replied the wise man. 'He is, and it doesn't make him less of a turkey.'

The prince took his words to heart and decided to wear a vest also. After some days the wise man called for a pair of trousers and said: 'Do you think that just because one is wearing trousers, a person cannot be a turkey?'

The prince agreed, and it went on like this until they were both fully dressed.

Some days later the wise man asked for some human food to be brought from the table: 'Do you think that just because one eats good food one cannot be a turkey?'

After the prince began to eat like a human being, the wise man asked: 'Do you imagine that there is a law that a turkey is only to sit under the table? It is possible to be a turkey and to sit at the table itself.' The prince accepted this, stood up, and walked about thereafter like a human being, behaving like one in every respect.

In this way, concluded Rabbi Nachman, the wise man healed him.

Complexity

This Hasidic tale touches on several aspects of relationships. At its core is the relationship between two human beings, a relationship established through silence, physicality and the intimacy of conversation. They find a way of being with each other, in a relationship of trust which enables the prince to establish a new relationship with himself, and his inner world, and thereby to re-forge a relationship with his outer world. This proto-therapeutic tale thus addresses the three overlapping areas in which our relationships occur: personal relationships with others; relationships with different aspects of ourselves; and relationships with our social setting and the outside world.

But the story is enigmatic in interesting ways. For example, it's unclear whether the prince stops believing he's a turkey. He doesn't appear to abandon his own idiosyncratic sense of self. He just ends his self-imposed separateness and his studied statement of difference, and agrees to re-engage with the world. Is this a gain or a loss? Who benefits from his return to relationships in the world of the royal court? It seems to suit the father more than the son. (And what was it about the relationship between parent and child that precipitated the son's need to enact his disdain for the parent's values in such a dramatic way?)

At the end of our story it may be the prince who has a more interesting relationship to his inner world than either the king or the wise man. For the prince knows he is a turkey *who is acting the part of a prince who is denying he is a turkey.* He is undeluded about who he is, whereas it is the wise man who is deluded if he thinks that he has cured the prince of his delusion. And it is the father who is deluded if he thinks his son now shares his view of the world.

It is a truism to say that relationships are complex. Relationships with those we say we love – and who say they love us. Relationships with parents and children; with partners and friends and colleagues; with the world; and with ourselves. We invest such a lot of emotionality in our relationships. But where is the spirituality? In the next section I would like to explore some of the ideas of Martin Buber, whose philosophy of relationship was central to his spiritual vision.

Buber's philosophy of relationship

Buber was born in Vienna in 1878. When he was three his parents separated, and he went to live with his grandparents in Galicia. The circumstances of his loss were never discussed, until one day he told a teenage childminder that he was missing his mother. Her response was a defining moment in his life:

> I can still hear her voice as she said, in a matter-of-fact way, 'No, your mother is not coming back any more.' I remember becoming silent. There was nothing more for me to say. But I felt that what she said was true, and the truth made me sad. I wanted to see my mother. And the impossibility of this gave me an infinite sense of deprivation and loss. Do you understand? Something had broken down. When I was 13 I even coined a private word for it, which had this meaning, a-meeting-that-had-gone-wrong (*Vergegnung*: 'mis-meeting/ miscounter') . . . Whatever I have learned in the course of my life about the meaning of meeting and dialogue between people springs from that moment when I was four.

Encounter with other people lies at the heart of Buber's spiritual philosophy of relationships. His yearning to connect with others in a real way may have stemmed from his early personal circumstances, but it was his encounter with Hasidism which enabled him to relate his philosophy to a wider framework of belief. The Hebrew word **hesed** – the root of the word **Hasid**ism – means lovingkindness, and Hasidism taught that God was encountered through actions between human beings, actions motivated by love.

According to Hasidic theosophy there is a divine spark in each human being. But this spark is surrounded by a kind of shell, which can be broken only by authentic acts in everyday life – acts from our deepest self. By acting with an attentive integrity of being, the divinity within us can be reached and expressed. In doing this we experience too the divinity within the world. As Buber saw it, the spiritual message of Hasidism was that

> Existence will remain meaningless for you if you yourself do not penetrate into it with active love and if you do not in this way discover its meaning for yourself. Everything is waiting to be hallowed by you . . . Meet the world with the fulness of your being and you shall meet God.

Buber transmuted these ideas into a personal philosophy of relationships. He believed there are two forms of relationship we can have with other people and the world around us. There is the 'I–Thou' way of relating and the 'I–It' way. And they are fundamentally different.

In an 'I–Thou' relationship one subject, 'I', relates to another subject, 'Thou'. This kind of relationship is characterised by openness, mutuality, directness, presentness: 'being with'. The 'I–It' relationship is characterised by the absence of these qualities. In an 'I–It' relationship we are relating to the world according to what it can do for us, and to other people as if they are objects.

The starting point for Buber's philosophy of relationships is thus not the human being in himself/herself. Nor is it the world out there. It's the relation *between* us and the world. We can relate to the world as 'Thou', or we can relate to the world as 'It'. It's as if there are two kinds of 'I' that we can inhabit. We have an 'I' capable of relating in a unique way to what is in front of us right now, an 'I' that is present in the moment, being with what is, as if for the first time. This 'I' is alive to the pristine quality of existence, its irreducible mysterious 'beingness', deeply strange and intimately familiar at the same time. Relating in this way, we meet the 'Thou' of the world.

But we also have an 'I' which observes, analyses, compares, classifies, arranges, appropriates. An 'I' that *uses* the world and other people within it. An isolated 'I' that stands outside the immediacy of experience – that is detached, cut off,

142

separate from the flow of being. Relating in this way, we meet the world of 'It'.

As you read these words you may remain distant from them, irritated, restless, disconnected. You may experience them, and the situation you find yourself in at this moment, in an 'I–It' way. Or, if you are fortunate, these words may reach across the gap between us. You may relate to them, and this moment when you encounter them, from a different part of yourself. You may meet this moment in an 'I–Thou' way.

Paying attention, 'being with' what is happening moment by moment, is impossible to sustain for very long at a time. Buber acknowledged that one cannot sustain an 'I–Thou' relationship indefinitely. Indeed one of the features of the 'I–Thou' relationship is its transience. It flows then ebbs, for in a way it is never repeatable, for the next time is another time. Something different will occur. Will it have the same quality of being? We do not – cannot – know. It is inevitable that every 'Thou' we encounter will turn into an 'It'. Nothing exists, according to Buber, that cannot become a 'Thou' for us, but inevitably it will withdraw sooner or later to the separation of an 'It'.

Buber stressed that the 'I–It' relationship isn't bad in itself, for it is only through 'I–It' relationships that objective knowledge is acquired and we can get on with the world of the everyday. It is the world of science, technology, the economy, but also of watching TV and queuing in supermarkets. Yet at every moment within these 'I–It' experiences there is the possibility that they can give way to an 'I–Thou' experience.

The Eternal Thou

Buber's philosophy of relationships was first described in his classic 1923 work *I and Thou*, where he writes of the three realms in which relation and encounter occur. There is nature, animate and inanimate; there is the interpersonal; and there is the world of art, knowledge and the intellect. In later years he expanded on these philosophical and spiritual ideas and tried to give practical examples of this twofold way of being in the world.

He once described an experience on his grandparents' estate with a favourite horse whom he'd loved to stroke. He felt its life beneath his hand, was aware of its ears flicking and its quiet snorting as it 'let me approach, confided itself to me, placed itself elementally in the relation of *Thou* to *Thou* with me'. Then one day 'it struck me about the stroking, what fun it gave me, and suddenly I became conscious of my hand. The game went on as before, but something had changed . . . And the next day, after giving him a rich feed, when I stroked my friend's head he did not raise his head.' Buber felt himself judged. He had moved from 'being with' the animal to using it for his own amusement. A subtle difference, but all the difference in the world: the difference between relating in an 'I–Thou' way and an 'I–It' way.

For Buber, paradise resides in our human encounter with what is presented to us moment by moment. Every 'I–Thou' meeting is in some sense a meeting with God: 'The lines of the I–Thou intersect in the eternal Thou.' Through our particular relationships in everyday life with people, animals, nature, art, technology, things in the world, this book in your hand, we can 'glimpse through to the Eternal Thou'. In meeting what we come across, what happens to us, with the fullness of our being, we encounter a mystery: the One(ness) that sustains existence.

Sport

Like a religion, a game seeks to codify and lighten
life. Played earnestly enough, a game can gather
to itself awesome dimensions of subtlety and
transcendental significance.

John Updike

'It's our religion ...'

The TV ad begins its stirring invocation, accompanied by
slow strings and massed choir: 'Life. It can be difficult. We
all know that. We all need someone to rely on. Someone
that makes you feel that you belong . . .' Meanwhile, on
the screen, in black-and-white images that Leni Riefenstahl
might have been proud of, there are ecstatic crowds, and
footballers' bodies-in-motion, and faces conveying joy and
anguish and despair. And then, with quickened voice and
throbbing, urgent beat: 'It's part of our history, part of our
country, and it *will* be part of our future. It's theatre, art, war
and love . . . It's a feeling that can't be explained but we
spend our lives explaining it. It's our religion.'

The new football season is heralded as a secular epiphany
worthy of our heart's devotion: 'They're our team, our

family, our life . . .' We are being invited to a communion and the ad is an appeal to the faithful, to the sports fan – from the Latin *fanaticus*: 'worshipper'.

Decades ago, when the American philosopher George Santayana was asked what he meant by the word 'religion', he replied 'another world to live in'. But when he said that he could not have anticipated how, for hundreds of millions of men and women throughout the world, what he meant by 'religion' would one day be displaced in the most immediate sense by organised spectator sports.

But this religion, this 'other world to live in', contains not God but numerous gods: reigning athletes of extraordinary (if sometimes ill-fated) gifts. This new religion is not a trans-cendental spiritual bond with a purposeful universe extracting from its believers rigours of conscience and behaviour, but an immanent dramatic bond sometimes sharply defined in terms of nationality, class or locality, at other times transcending race, religion, gender, class, nationality. Venus Williams and Earvin 'Magic' Johnson and Tiger Woods and Cathy Freeman and David Beckham – each of them majestically accomplished in their chosen sport – have entered a new transglobal pantheon, attracting to them devotees whose lives are significantly influenced by the fluctuating fortunes of these luminous presences.

The decline of religion as a source of significant meaning in modern societies, as an organising principle in people's lives, has been extravagantly compensated for by the rise of popular culture in general. The billion-dollar sports-mania is just the most visible manifestation of this. The proselytising ambitions of the new religion are as ruthless as any of the old religions. Sport is a new source of values. And sport has infiltrated into areas of life where previously it had no presence.

For example, sport is no longer, as it used to be, over-whelmingly male. When Brandi Chastain whipped off her shirt in the Rose Bowl stadium in Los Angeles after scoring the winning goal for the United States in the 1999 Women's World Cup final – revealing in the process her Nike-sponsored bra – she did so in front of more than 90,000 football fans gathered from around the world (more than watched the 1998 France–Brazil World Cup final in Paris). Another 40 million watched on television around the country. Women's football is the fastest growing team sport in the world.

Concurrent with this we find that sport is no longer lowbrow, and stuck on the back page of newspapers. It's become the stuff of serious literary endeavour. The American author Don Delillo's remarkable novel *Underworld* (1997) opens with a sixty-page bravura description of the legendary World Series game played in New York in 1951 between the Dodgers and the Giants: four Cold War decades of American history – 'all falling indelibly into the past' (like our own lives) – filtered through the prism of a single game of baseball.

In its finest manifestations, sport has created a new planetary language in which disciplined physical activity combines with spontaneous instinct to enact moments of spiritual grandeur. At these moments the human body becomes a vehicle for the celebration of the human spirit (see chapter on Bodies). Through sport (like sex), bodily self-expression can render the soul transparent.

Grace

As more and more people do sports – and experience the moments of self-transcendence which religious devotion once offered – so too more and more of us watch sports. For the sports fan the team, or idolised individual player, provides a kind of externalised soul: there to be celebrated, but – as the God of the ages apparently was not – there in full public view.

Manchester United football club sells replica shirts which

have just one word printed on the back above the number 7: *Dieu*. 'God' here is a reference to the team's dominant player of the 1990s, Eric Cantona, whose charisma on and off the field assured the enigmatic Frenchman a permanent place in the impassioned folk-memory of the club.

In 1997, the year of Cantona's retirement, a north of England artist, Michael Browne, exhibited in the Manchester Gallery of Art his large-scale painting (based on a famous work by Caravaggio) in which the original figure of the resurrected Christ surrounded by Pontius Pilate and Roman soldiers was replaced by the figure of Cantona, with the United manager and some of the younger players from the team standing in for the original onlookers.

Adulation and adoration on this scale is telling us something about the deep human need which we all have – a spiritual need – for special figures who can represent for us certain ideals and values, and who can give us access to moments of joy, of rapture, to visionary moments of the sublime, to a sense that the old religious categories of mystery and wonder and awe are momentarily present within our desacralised world.

Those of us who watch certain players' poised authority and *élan*, their proudly humble artfulness on the pitch (or chosen sporting arena), are exposed to moments of exhilarating intensity akin to the ecstasy described in medieval religious mystical literature. At certain moments the world becomes illuminated by another dimension of being. We did not know that playing a game could allow us this glimpse of grace.

'Theatre, art . . .'

Sport's theatricality releases in us deep emotions. Think of the catharsis when we are finally released from the inner tension generated in some games between the excitement and hope for victory and the fear of imminent defeat. And defeat is by far the most common experience for players and fans alike. Defeat is built into the structure of competitive sports in a particular way: only one team can win the Cup, only one player can win gold. The rest have to face the poignancy of loss, the pain of mourning, of waking up the next morning knowing what might have been, but isn't. It's gone. Like a death, like the failed dreams in our lives, defeat scars the soul over and over again with the awareness that failure and loss are unavoidable aspects of our shared human condition.

Traditionally religion – that 'other way of seeing' – taught that our souls can be hurt but not destroyed, that something of us does survive even the ending we call death. In the religion that is sport, the pain of defeat and loss are faced, lived through, and survived: there is, after all, next year (or just the next game). Hope can be renewed. The consolations provided for the religious believer by the hereafter, the world to come, are transferred over time to the new season. The disappointment of past losses can be dulled by thoughts of what glory there might be in that eagerly awaited, not too distant, future.

But unlike theatre – where plays have scripts, and one knows that Lear always dies at the end – competitive sports have no prepared script. However rehearsed are the players in skills and tactics, what generates passion in the viewer is the unmediated experience of spontaneity, of the unpredictable, of living moment by moment not knowing what will happen next. This is where the experience of watching (or playing) sports can be seen to intersect with the spiritual understanding which grows out of acknowledging that there is no knowing, no controlling, what life will reveal next. Sport is the incarnation of the fluidity of being.

We recall that *Adonai* is process, the Hebrew Bible's 'God'-word meaning 'that-which-is'. The unexpectedness of what can occur, moment by moment, within a sporting encounter gives its watchers a kind of secular spiritual experience: we can experience in a concentrated form the extraordinary mystery – which we might glimpse only rarely during the rest of our lives – of life unfolding, intricately, unrepeatably, before our wondering eyes.

In the 1995 final of soccer's European Cup Winners' Cup, one could sit through a tense, unfolding drama of a match, over two hours long, up to its final 30 seconds, when in one moment of unimaginable spontaneity, of consternation and wonder, a moment which caused overwhelming joy or heart-wrenching despair depending on which team you supported, the Spaniard Nayim lobbed the ball from the halfway line in a long, looping arc, which soared and rose and then, breathtakingly, plummeted beyond the desperately retreating Arsenal goalkeeper into the net to win the match for Zaragoza.

For supporters of these two teams, moments like these become etched in the mind far more powerfully and long-lastingly than anything conventional religion can offer. They teach of sorrow, or thankfulness; of how in one moment one's life can turn from hope to despair, or despair to gratitude; of how one action, or one moment of vision, can transform one's destiny. The spiritual significance of football becomes revealed within these unrepeatable moments.

Unrepeatable? Here we have a difference between watching sport in person and watching on television. The experience in the flesh can open us to feelings which we may be sorely missing in our own lives: the experience of community, of unity, of shared purpose. Some of this is experienced by the TV viewer too, but what television does in addition is allow us to revisit these moments of inspiration. And sometimes it is only by revisiting, re-watching, these moments that their beauty can properly be enjoyed and understood.

Watching sport on TV can make us realise how painful it is sometimes that we cannot replay or freeze-frame our own lives. Our moments of joy, of inspiration, of awe, of pleasure, can never be revisited, never recaptured. Photos, videos, may provide us with memories, but in that distance between the past and the present there is the unspeakable knowledge of loss, the pain of time's arrow, which flies in one direction only. 'Time's winged chariot' speeds us on, to the grave. There is no going back. The past is unrecoverable, un-revisitable. There are no action replays of the lives we lead. This is part of the harshness of human existence. We live within an irreversible current of time in which our actions do have consequences, and these consequences cannot be undone.

And what of 'art'? If we recall in our mind's eye the almost supernatural acuity of Andre Agassi's strokeplay, or the pre-ternatural grandiloquence of Michael Johnson's sprinting, or the unbearably fragile gracefulness of the young Olga Korbut's gymnastics, then we know that through such manifestations of the human spirit we are witnessing numinosity in action. That we poor human beings, in all our frailty, are capable of creating moments that touch the soul of others, moments of eternity – whether the medium is music or art or sport – this creative spirit is a mystery, beyond analysis. At these moments we may become aware of our mysterious connection to that creative Spirit which animates all of existence, that energy with a thousand names, manifestations of 'being-and-becoming'.

> An artist, in my eyes, is someone who can lighten up a dark room. I have never and will never find any difference between the pass from Pelé to Carlos Alberto in the final of the World Cup in 1970 and the poetry of the young Rimbaud, who stretches 'cords from steeple to steeple and garlands from window to window'. There is in each of these human manifes-tations an expression of beauty which touches us and gives us a feeling of eternity.
>
> *Eric Cantona*

' . . . war and love . . .'

'War' we understand. From time to time, in almost all sports, a minority of fans can become so overwhelmed by the passions aroused by their devotion that violence erupts, a primitive outpouring of cursing, abuse and physical violence which can cast a deep shadow over the sport itself: 'weekend Taliban'. But although sport can occasion the hateful excesses of nationalism, chauvinism and xenophobia, this shouldn't sour us to the spiritual potential within this bizarre adventure in the human spirit. We yearn to feel a sense of belonging. And sport provides this: a secular faith community, a community in which we can celebrate joyful moments and receive solace for our pain. A community with shared beliefs and ideals. 'All that I know most surely about morality and obligations, I owe to football' (Albert Camus, writer and goalkeeper).

Sport is the benign, creative counterpart of war. Although sport generates in us elemental passions, it offers us opportunities for the control of aggression in the service of something grander. In fact, success in competitive sports necessitates the transformation of aggression into creative rather than destructive channels. For sport provides a model of the capacity in human beings to control, discipline and redirect their innate aggressive feelings into moments of inspiration and creativity.

And what of 'love'? The men, women and teams who become the finest, the most skilful, exponents of their chosen disciplines do evoke in those who follow them emotional bonds as passionate as any in human experience – not excluding marriage and family. Sport, like love, can drive us crazy with desire. For anyone whose daily life and working week revolves around thoughts about their chosen player or team; who has travelled hundreds of miles just to watch their sporting heroes in action for some brief period of time; who has paid exorbitant prices to see them perform;

who has stood on open terraces in driving rain ... such madness is the madness that only lovers know. A divine madness, a mystery that surpasses rational understanding, a mystery of the spirit.

Truth

It is better to believe in the hard idea of truth than the facile idea of sincerity.

Iris Murdoch

The truth is often a terrible weapon of aggression. It is possible to lie, and even to murder, for the truth.

Alfred Adler

There is no truth, only interpretations

Nietzsche

What is truth?

Truths sometimes come at us from unexpected angles. I heard recently about the college lecturer who, after many failed attempts, finally managed to arrange with the Chinese authorities a trip to Tibet. He wanted to lead a party of UK students to the renowned Jokhang temple in Lhasa in order to meet the monks and learn something of the spiritual richness of their Buddhist way of life. Such opportunities for spiritual enlightenment are rare and after a 16–day trip he and his students eventually reached this holy shrine on the roof of the world. There they received the honour of being granted an audience with the revered head monk. Somewhat in awe, the lecturer approached him, nervously wondering what eternal truth would be revealed to him. The spiritual head of the temple leaned over and whispered: 'I think . . . David Beckham is the best footballer on the planet . . .'

What spiritual truths do we think we need to know? What truths are we wanting revealed to us? Is it the grand truths that capture our attention – about the purpose of life, good and evil, God, suffering and death? Or are we more interested in the intimate truths, the everyday truths – the truth about ourselves, about our relationships and their vicissitudes, about why happiness may elude us, why discontent shadows our being? Or maybe we sense that these two kinds of truth are not so far apart, that perhaps the big questions and the little questions are two sides of the same coin. That the intricacy of one's personal truth – what one has been, what one has done, what one is, what one is doing – is a microcosm of the largest questions a human being can ask.

Truthfulness is a mirror in which the spiritual becomes visible. We sense that paying attention to 'that which is', without too much defensiveness or wishfulness, leads us deeper into the mystery of being. That if we have the courage, the tenacity, the resourcefulness, to reflect diligently on what unfolds within us, around us and between us, moment by moment, we may come near to the truth of things. How things 'really' are, rather than how we would like them to be. Or fear them to be. Or how we're told that they are.

For how reliable is what we're told? Pilate's question to Jesus – 'What is truth?' (John 18:38) – is not (only) disingenuous. Truths are a dime a dozen. We are assailed by truths and truth-tellers: politicians, religious leaders, parents, psychologists, lawyers, teachers, academics, advertisers, military leaders, economists, technocrats, scientists, accountants, consultants, commentators, an endless flow of authorities and 'experts' who claim that what they have to tell us is 'true'. But which stories are we to believe? Whose 'truths' are trustworthy?

Objective and subjective truth

We desperately want truth to be out there: to be solid, substantial, objective. We want the security of knowing how things are. We search for truth as if it is encoded in creation in a script we can learn to read. As if it is waiting for us to discover or decipher – or just to stumble across. We wish that truth had the hard, shiny, revelatory quality of some pre-existing object, like the solid black monoliths in Stanley Kubrick's *2001: A Space Odyssey*. Or the irreducible facticity of the periodic table of chemical elements, as discovered by the young Oliver Sacks when he first visited London's Science Museum when it reopened in 1945 after the war:

> In that first, long, rapt encounter . . . I was convinced that the periodic table [inscribed in large letters on the wall] was neither arbitrary nor superficial, but a representation of truths which would never be overturned, but would, on the contrary, continually be confirmed, show new depths with new knowledge, because it was as deep and simple as nature itself. And the perception of this produced in my twelve-year-old self a sort of ecstasy, the sense (in Einstein's words) that 'a corner of the great veil had been lifted'.

Like the awesome beauty of certain mathematical equations, scientific truths have their own spiritual grandeur. Sacks, like Einstein before him, experienced the world as it is in itself, its construction radiating the numinous. Such truths can provide life with a sense of meaning as surely as can the ecstasy of the mystic or the vision of the prophets.

Yet life still has to be lived – after the ecstasy, after the vision – in the diffuse and uncertain light of the everyday. Such truths as Oliver Sacks encountered, never to be overturned, are the envy of those of us non-scientists who seek truth in the intangible day-to-day realm of the spiritual. For spiritual 'truths' are rarely incontrovertible. Like religious, philosophical and psychological truths, they interpret reality, creating a language to describe, subjectively, how things can be seen to be. They are cultural constructs and although they can inspire devotion or gratitude or humility, although they can enhance or even transform our felt experience of life, they do not have the down-to-earth exactness of value-neutral scientific representations of how things are. Spiritual truths lack the definitiveness, the vocabulary of precision, of the scientific world view.

Spiritual truth cannot be grasped like a diamond. It is not a present we can wrap up and take home. Nor is it a security-blanket in which we can wrap ourselves up out of harm's way. I distrust luminous, revelatory truths that drop from the skies, or the lips of experts, or are induced at moments of heightened emotionality. Such truths may claim for themselves the solidity of the physical sciences but they are imaginative exercises. And when the spiritual truths revealed by the boundless, fertile human imagination become doctrinal or ideological they betray the fluidity of being. 'The truth is a snare: you cannot have it, without being caught. You cannot have the truth in such a way that you catch it, but only in such a way that it catches you' (Søren Kierkegaard).

Speaking truthfully

We are told that the truth will set us free. But which truth is that? The Talmud describes truth as 'God's seal': when we reach the truth of things we decipher a signature engraved within the world. We glimpse the coherence of being. We discover an alignment with *Adonai*, 'that which is'. This is one kind of spiritual truth. It is the truth alluded to in the Jewish morning service, in the ancient daily reminder: 'At all times a person can/should be in awe of the divine . . . acknowledging *the truth* and speaking *the truth* within themselves.'

In the Hebrew, to 'acknowledge' the truth involves gratitude. One recognises that there is a stratum of being – how things are in themselves – which exists independently of our perception of it: we can be thankful that truth is not only what we decide is true. But the prayer repeats the word '*truth*'. It moves from a notion of objective truth to subjective truth: 'speaking *the truth within ourselves*'. This is the truth that 'catches' us – sometimes by surprise.

'This above all: to thine own self be true.' Although the advice to Hamlet is offered by Polonius – a character whose rhetoric is suspect – Shakespeare's humanist injunction–admonition leaves everything open and resonant. It seems to offer endless opportunity for optimism, for the spiritual adventure of self-discovery.

Yet isn't being 'true to ourselves' the mantra of the age we live in? It can have the self-centred, discordant tone of a child banging endlessly on a tin drum. And how do we know what being 'true to ourselves' means? The unconscious is a great subverter of the truth claims we make. Our capacity for self-deception is enormous.

Furthermore, the idea of truth can become idolatrous and coercive. We may find ourselves submitting to a view of ourselves that we've come to believe is true: perhaps what we've figured 'must' be true about ourselves; or what someone else has told us about ourselves. Either way we can get trapped into conforming to (or living up to) false formulations about who we are, who our self is to whom we have to 'be true'. The hallmark of truthfulness of perception is the recognition of the implausibility of these kinds of definitive statements and self-descriptions. Being true to ourselves may turn out to mean being true to a deep understanding of our own incoherence. That we can never know ourselves well enough to refract more than a provisional truth at a particular moment in time.

The American existential psychoanalyst Leslie Farber wrote wisely and directly in the 1970s about the questionable nature of the search for truth (in psychoanalysis and in life): 'The truth that interests me is problematical, partial, modest – and still breathing. It is not normally dramatic or revelatory, and its attainment depends far more on thinking hard than feeling freely. To put it another way: I think that speaking truthfully is a more fitting ambition than speaking the truth.'

This is salutary: the quest for self-knowledge, psychological or spiritual, can lead to falseness rather than truth.

Living on the tightrope

So where does that leave us? Maybe with the Psalmist: 'Truth springs out of the earth . . .' (Psalm 85:12). In other words truth is not above our heads, faraway, grandiose, eternal. It doesn't come from heaven, ready-made. It is, rather, that which actively comes into being, sprouting close to hand. It is down-to-earth, local, gestating, abundant, fragile. Truth grows organically out of the ground of our experience. We can nurture it and protect it, in the spirit of Martin Buber: 'The truth belongs to God alone. But there is a human truth, namely, to be devoted to the truth.' We can tend it, attend to it, but we can't manufacture it, own it, possess it.

For those for whom religious truths are sacred, this will be a scary, perhaps inadmissible, prospect. We long for the security of knowing we have the truth within our grasp. We long for the ease of answers, the stability that comes from certainty, the splendour and intensity of feeling which accompanies the ownership of truth. It is far from easy to have to wrestle truth from the givenness of being. But any spiritual truth that's worth having will partake of the ordinary, fragmentary nature of being: 'The true way leads along a tightrope, which is not stretched aloft but just above the ground. It seems designed more to trip one than to be walked along.' (Franz Kafka)

Kafka found himself – to his distress – devoted to speaking truthfully. But through his ordeal he gifted us enlightenment. His words make transparent the enigmatic quality of truth. To live spiritual truth, 'just above the ground', is to become an acrobat of the soul. At every moment we risk becoming destabilised. We may well fall flat on our face. Speaking truthfully is a balancing act that requires our full attention.

Uncertainty

The whole world is a very narrow bridge, but the
essential thing is not to be afraid, at all

Nachman of Bratslav

Fear

But how can we not be afraid? In the face of the unac-
ceptability of the world – the unpredictable threats of
terrorist attack, the potential for globalised economic in-
stability, the invisible encroachment of environmental
suicide – let alone the threats to our well-being through
illness, crime, the breakdown of family life, the inevitability
of our own deaths, in the face of all this collective and
personal uncertainty how can we not be afraid?

In the face of the world's demands and terrors, what could
it mean that 'the essential thing is not to be afraid, at all'?
For maybe fear is a healthy response. Fear doesn't always
paralyse; it can jolt us out of inaction, complacency,
resignation. If we are frightened it suggests that we value
life, that we recognise its fragility, its impermanence: we
register in our body, in our guts, our pounding heart, our
trembling hands, that faced by the absurd transience of all

161

flesh we do care, care desperately, about our mortal selves and what we make of our lives.

When we feel insecure what we desire more than anything else is reassurance. We search for the security that comes from certainty. But where are we to find it? The temptation is to beat a retreat from disorder and suffering and embrace the comfort (illusory but gratifying) of traditional answers and values. The certitudes of one dogmatic faith or another are always present, the safety of '-isms' and a world ordered according to a revelation that has already been handed down. Capitalism, communism, Freudianism, consumerism, environmentalism, religious fundamentalism, fascism, socialism, Marxism: this last century has seen a host of movements and theories which cater for the deep human need for certainty. Structures of thought and frameworks for living which rescue us from chaos and doubt. Ambivalence and uncertainties are abolished in the light of the truth of the '-ism'.

But the consequences are grim. The germ of violence and repression which is latent in all dogma can attack us unawares. We soon find ourselves reacting with the same intolerance we're so quick to condemn in others. Open-mindedness, tolerance of difference, humaneness, *menschlichkeit* – qualities which we have to struggle over and over again to achieve within ourselves – collapse back into opinions, attitudes, beliefs and actions that are narrow, polarised and defensive. Our inner ghetto. For we do grow afraid: feelings of uncertainty – of not being sure what to think, not knowing the answers, not understanding what is really going on – are hard to tolerate.

And when we grow afraid we fail to maintain that delicate balancing act which embraces 'both . . . and . . .', a psychological balancing act which is a spiritual discipline. Instead we fall back into the 'either . . . or . . .' of the human being's earliest experiences of life. So: either mummy is holding me, feeding me, being with me, comforting me, and I love her and I feel secure and I am gaining a sense of who I am, loveable and worthwhile, and this is paradise; or I am cold and hungry and angry and in distress and feel neglected and I hurt and I hate and I feel fragmented and I am in hell. As infants we oscillated between these kinds of experiences. Our capacity as adults to tolerate the inevitable insecurities and uncertainties we encounter is influenced by how well we survived and negotiated these early infantile states of mind.

Experiencing the world in this emotionally cartoon-like fashion, splitting the world into simple dichotomies – love and hate, good and evil, friends and enemies, believers and non-believers, us or them, my way or else – does provide a kind of security. But the consolations of pseudo-clarity and fabricated certainty are a spiritual defeat. The triumph of death over life. The defeat of the question by the answer. Questions are acts of resistance against the totalitarianism of certainty. To maintain a stance of benign questioning in the face of the world's pull towards the security of the familiar, the safety of the known, involves a recognition that ambivalence and uncertainty can be spiritual assets.

They can lead us towards depth, towards complexity, towards vitality, towards a glimpse of *Adonai*, the One who is all. The One who/which embraces opposites in a unity that human consciousness can never embrace. And offers a sense of oneness through which one can momentarily be embraced.

'Negative Capability'

This openness to ambivalence, ambiguity, complexity and uncertainty does require a certain fearlessness. One has to know – but how can one know? – that one won't fall off the narrow bridge, descend into madness, disintegrate emotionally, damage ourselves irreparably. Can we face the risk?

The 22–year-old medical student John Keats had just

published his first volume of poetry when, in December 1817, he wrote to his brothers about the quality of inwardness necessary for personal achievement, particularly literary achievement: 'I mean Negative Capability, that is, when a man is capable of being in uncertainties, mysteries, doubts without any irritable reaching after fact and reason.' Keats had Shakespeare in mind when he attempted to describe this emotional-intellectual-spiritual capacity which can lead to creative achievement. But he was highlighting something which has broader application.

He seems to be describing a particular state of mind, or state of being, in which the need for supposedly objective truth – 'fact and reason' – is temporarily suspended in favour of a different stance, a being with ('being in') what is not yet known, what is not yet grasped clearly, what is not yet understood. He is suggesting a more free-floating mode of perception, a looser, almost dream-like way of being which allows 'what is' to arise in its own way and in its own time and in its own idiosyncratic shape. A mode of being which permits some space to become empty, momentarily, so that something can come into it which is not yet known about.

This mode of being, this not-knowing-so-that-something-new-can-become-known, tolerates doubt and uncertainty for long enough for the unconscious (the gods, one's muse, the self) to speak, to reveal, to communicate, to form itself in thought. It is the stance underpinning artistic creativity, scientific discovery, daydreaming, psychoanalytic interpretation, spiritual contemplation: a mode of attunement in which something new is uncovered or revealed – a fresh idea, a novel form of words, an original thought, an inspirational insight, a solution to a seemingly intractable problem, an opening up of a way forward.

It is the stance too of the storyteller and the interpreter of texts and all who recognise that life is polymorphous and relentless with meaning.

Walking the tightrope

A group of Hasidim were once seated together, when Rabbi Israel of Rizhyn joined them, his pipe in his hand. They asked him: 'Rabbi, how should we serve God?'

He was surprised at the question and replied: 'How should I know?' But then he went on talking and told them this story:

There were two friends and both were accused before the king of a crime. Since the king loved them, he wanted to show them mercy, but he could not acquit them because even the king's word cannot prevail over a law. So he gave this verdict: A rope was to be stretched across a deep chasm and the two were to walk it, one after the other. Whoever reached the other side was to be granted his life.

The rope was set up and the first of the friends got safely across. The other cried to him: 'Tell me how you managed to cross?' The first called back: 'I don't know anything except this: whenever I felt myself toppling over to one side, I leaned to the other.'

What do we make of this? Firstly, these two unnamed individuals might be strangers to us but they are not strangers to each other. They are 'friends'. So this is a story about friendship: about the potential that friendship gives for companionship, advice and support in the face of the world's trials. We are not always alone. We are allowed to be dependent. We need each other. Such support can, on occasions, be lifesaving.

The two friends stand 'accused before the king of a crime'. We aren't told what they've done. We never find out. Are they innocent or guilty? Is the accusation just or unjust? We don't know. We recall that disturbing opening sentence, both comic and nightmarish, of Kafka's *The Trial*: 'Someone must have been telling lies about Joseph K., for without having done anything wrong he was arrested one fine morning.' This is paradigmatic of the uncertainty we face daily.

165

As in the Hasidic story and Kafka, nobody tells us what we have done wrong. And yet often we feel on trial. We berate ourselves for our failures to live as we should – or as we've been told we should. Do the accusations relate to our real wrongdoings? Or are they relics of old rules we've failed to outgrow? Often we accuse ourselves for our very humanity – for all those quirks and peccadilloes that accompany us on our journeys and make us who we are.

Then suddenly in the story, in the face of the accusation, there is love. But the king's love (or God's love, or our own human capacity to love) is not enough. Love does not conquer all. Love alone cannot produce a merciful acquittal. This king is not omnipotent: 'even the king's word cannot prevail over a law'. It seems that the universe we live in is ordered in ways that cannot change 'what is' in order to fit in with our needs or wishes. Things are the way that they are. But in the midst of how they are there is an opportunity for each individual to take responsibility in the face of the uncertainties. We are tested.

The test: a traditional folklore motif. The tightrope is in place. The chasm lies below. The first friend gets safely across. The one who remains – and do we not think of ourselves as the one who remains, as the one who stands wondering how others manage to navigate their way through the vicissitudes of life? – cries out: 'How did you manage to do that?' And the enigmatic response is ours to unravel: 'I don't know anything except this: whenever I felt myself toppling over to one side, I leaned to the other.'

'How do I know?'

Is this a parable about avoiding extremes? About the importance of leading what we so nonchalantly call a 'balanced' life? Is it about paying precise attention, moment by moment, to what we are doing? About making all those small adjustments and sensitive responses to what life presents us with? So many questions are raised by this final sentence. Is it possible to help someone else by sharing one's own experience? Is how the first friend survived the journey across the chasm of any relevance to how the second will need to do it? Maybe the significant part of what is said by the survivor is in admitting that how they survived can't really be communicated fully: 'I don't know anything . . .'

The story ends abruptly. We don't know if the friend who still has to walk the tightrope will manage to get across. And if they do, how they will do it. Yet that feels right. For these two friends are like two parts of ourselves. One part of us has had experiences where we have feared we would fall: into despondency, or a sense of meaninglessness, or a rage without end, or into despair about our lives. And yet we have survived, and maybe on looking back we feel: 'I don't know how I did it.' So one part of us has crossed chasms, and we are intact, more or less. But another part feels and knows almost nothing of this. A part of us still stands rooted to the spot, knowing we have it all still to do: tasks ahead that we feel we are completely unable to achieve, choices to make that we don't know how we are going to make. From this side of the chasm everything may indeed look bleak, or terrifying, or hopeless. How are we going to manage?

This parable of the two friends is of course a story within a story. It's Rabbi Israel's response to the teasing question: 'How should we serve God?' Perhaps surprisingly, we hear first his acceptance that one doesn't know, definitively, the answer to that question. But in the absence of clear answers, in the absence of any simple and immediate knowing what is right, what God wants – in the absence, in other words, of a fundamentalist's response – there are still things we can say. First of all we can tell stories. This is our human attempt to address the mysteries of life through image and metaphor, through art.

In our capacity to create stories, to weave out of language these fragile nets of meaning to catch us as we fall, in this narrative capacity of ours we are exercising that part of ourselves which is divine. Within the Judaic myth, God's attempt at storytelling (as it were) is contained in the Torah. God speaks – and the world comes into being. Our human storytelling is inspired by the image we have of God's self-disclosure within the Torah. We speak – and create worlds of our own. We might not 'know' – but we can tell stories.

And in this Hasidic story, Rabbi Israel's own not-knowing is not the end of the story, but the beginning of a new story. His acceptance of uncertainty, his 'being in . . . doubts', allows something else to open up. And similarly with the one who at the end calls out 'I don't know anything except this . . .' First there is not-knowing, uncertainty. And from there something new can arise. A story about personal experience, felt experience: 'This is what I went through: in the face of uncertainty, I tried to pay enough attention to what I was doing moment by moment that I could respond to what was demanded of me. I offer you this, wholeheartedly, in friendship . . .'

An acceptance of uncertainty; attentiveness; openness; personal disclosure; companionship; storytelling. Do these add up to a form of spiritual practice? Something that used to be called 'the service of God'?

Vanity

Vanity of vanities, all is vanity . . .

Ecclesiastes 1:2

Emptiness

Vanity is all around us. From the seduction of newspaper 'lifestyle' supplements to the self-promoting posturing of pseudo-'personalities'. From self-deluding pride in how hard we work, how much stress we endure, how much sex we enjoy, to the self-serving preening of the entertainment and fashion industries. From the moment we wake up in the morning and check our image in the mirror, to last thing at night when we apply our creams and potions to stop the body's decay. Vanity: from the Latin *vanitas* – 'emptiness'. But what is this emptiness we do not wish to feel? What anxieties are we trying to efface?

UK consumers spend £500million a year on cosmetics. Women, and increasingly men, who feel the need to enhance or disguise their appearances, to cover up or transform themselves. What self-contempt is our vanity attempting to hide? What could give us the security within ourselves to know who we are without depending on the

169

props of looks and clothes, where we holiday or shop? What inner malaise are we suffering from that we put such store on outer things?

Perhaps the ubiquity of homogenised global brands provides a clue. For brands have become powerful social forces, colonising our hearts and minds. Physically intrusive and spiritually invasive, brands bypass our cynicism. We have great affection for them and loyalty to them. We'll pay over the odds for the logo: Adidas, Swatch, Calvin Klein offer us consistency of quality and points of certainty in an uncertain world. Religion can't compete with that. Brands now generate more trust than most institutions. Governments, politicians, religious leaders, schoolteachers, scientists – the traditional sources of authority – all fall before the credibility and dependability of the leading brands. They are the crutch which helps us know who we are. Vainly we clutch at them.

From where do they derive their power over us? Is it because we no longer identify so strongly with our nation, our religion, our political party, our local community? As if there's some basic insecurity within us, so we latch on to the familiarity and predictability of certain omnipresent consumer items. As if there's some deep crisis of the self and we've begun to construct our sense of who we are through our association with brands – from football teams to TV channels, from designer clothes to the make of our car, from cosmetics to coffee shops. The security of knowing we are not alone.

The power of brands

Brand advertising is ubiquitous, brilliant and subversive. It taps into our deepest fears. Take L'Oréal's slogan: 'Because you're worth it'. In a world where you can feel just another faceless statistic in the bureaucratic machine, where you can feel yourself teetering on the edge of worthlessness, where no amount of consumer rights or technological innovations can conquer the anomie at the heart of societies that fail to generate spiritual depth and personal meaning – who wouldn't want to feel that you were being given something 'because you're worth it'?

Although this is the message that traditional religions once promoted – that you were a unique human being, with a soul, a divine spark within, that you were precious and valuable, of infinite worth just because you were here on earth, suffused with the spirit of being, alive and vital – we can now get that sense of worth over the counter. In a world where human life itself is dispensable (see the daily news), the message that you can buy your sense of worth soothes disturbing inner doubts about our purpose here on earth.

Brands have moved on from being simply about the qualities of the product or service they sell. They are now promoted as a set of values, a philosophy, an ideology of life. Orange represents a bright, optimistic future in which there can be real 'communication' between people. Nike is about individuality and personal achievements. Traditional religious values of honesty, dedication, friendship, human connectedness have been co-opted, secularized, repackaged and sold back to us. We no longer gain our integrity through a lifetime's work on our souls, but by buying Benetton.

When brands take on a good cause – like AIDS or the death penalty – they are seeking to legitimize the corporation as a morally and socially responsible institution. In doing so they are pandering to our vanity: our own wish to be seen as morally and socially responsible people. Through possession of the brand we can experience the kudos of being associated with goodness – but without the effort involved.

They are also hoping that we will forget the downsizing, the sweatshop wages, the environmental waste, the huge pay inequalities between the boardroom and the shop floor. What we're being sold is meaning and purpose, along with a sense of identity and a sense of belonging. Spiritual needs sold off-the-peg to souls craving for salvation. Salvation from doubt, from fear, from the deepest questions about who we are and why we are here.

The vanity of ownership replaces the humility of recognising our smallness and impermanence. The vanity of possessions and looks and spurious achievements replaces the humbling acknowledgement that we come from the dust and return to the dust. The key word for brand consultants is 'belief'. A whole language has sprung up: brand bible, brand heaven, brand soul. This is the closest many people get to a religious world view. The evidence is that this is what is longed for – readily accessible pre-fabricated meaning. As soon as you link even basic products like food or shampoo to a metaphysical or spiritual idea the consumer will buy into it. To the extent that traditional religions in the West have failed to impart their essential values in ways to which we can relate, in the resulting vacuum we experience a spiritual thirsting after meaning and purpose, and an emotional hunger to feel good about ourselves.

'Vanity of vanities . . .'

'I have seen all the activities that go on in the world and, really, everything is vanity and spiritual vexation' (Ecclesiastes 1:14). The author of the most pessimistic book in the Bible is not only world-weary and cynical. The author is also depressed: there is a despair and anger within the book that gives it a strangely contemporary feel. As if Kafka and Tom Wolfe had joined forces. From the opening refrain onwards the key word is the Hebrew *hevel*: vanity, futility, triviality, emptiness. More emptiness.

The author's sadness and frustration echoes through the book. 'I said inside myself: "Go on then, I'll prove there's such a thing as happiness; I'll have a good time", but it was all *hevel* – in vain, futile, empty' (2:1). 'And I said to myself: "Whatever can happen to a fool can also happen to me; so why do I think I'm so clever?" Then I admitted to myself: whatever one does – it's *hevel*' (2:15).

One of the things that I find inspirational about the biblical canon is that it doesn't disguise the anguish of being human. It holds within itself salient doubts about whether life has any meaning or purpose or value. It gives voice to hopelessness and despair. This radical motif runs through the literature of the Hebrew Bible as a counterpoint to the dominant tone of optimism and purposefulness about creation. The Judaic emphasis on the centrality and worth of the individual, our mutual interdependence, the need for responsible action, our interrelationship with an energy that animates all being – all of this articulates a powerful message of hopefulness and possibility. But threaded through these multifarious narratives are subdued recognitions that human life on earth is also nasty, brutish and short. And that our pitiful vanity is one way we protect ourselves from this knowledge.

'What is our life?'

This consciousness of our innate vulnerability – and our vulnerability to delusions of invulnerability – appears too in later Jewish texts. The daily morning prayers contain material designed to help us face our inconsequentiality, to accept our limitations, to see ourselves as we are: that our mortality is not an opportunity for self-promotion but an opportunity for promoting self-inquiry. One text reads:

> What are we? What is our life? What is our love? What is our justice? What is our success? What is our endurance? What is our power? What can one say in the presence of *Adonai*, our God present and past? In relation to you are not the powerful as nothing, the famous as if they had never existed, the learned as if without knowledge, and the intelligent as if without insight? For most of our actions are pointless *(tohu)*

and our daily life is *hevel*, empty, shallow, vanity. Even the superiority of humanity over the beasts is nothing, for everything is *hevel*: empty, insubstantial, in vain. Except the pure soul . . .

Poignant and demanding, the prayer asks us to reflect on our transience. Living a life replete with questions penetrates our imagined omniscience and punctures our vain pretensions. In relation to all that exists, in the light of the divine superfluity of being which infuses creation, most of our actions are 'pointless'. The Hebrew word *tohu* points us back to the creation myth in Genesis where, before the divine spirit creates order out of chaos, the earth is described as *tohu va'vohu*: unformed and void (see the chapter on Creativity).

Its appearance in our text presents us with a paradox. On the one hand it recalls how insubstantial are any of our vaunted achievements. On the other hand it reminds us that all is not lost: if our actions share this primeval quality of formlessness then something durable and precious can emerge from us. Most of what we do may be unformed, without yet having any 'point', but creation – divine and human – arises from the midst of this chaotic state of being.

But this ray of hopefulness doesn't last long. It can easily lead to hubris and the adoption of an inflated view of our own importance. So the text immediately rubs home the vanity with which we attribute significance to our actions. It does this by means of an ironic refutation of the whole thrust of the Genesis creation myth, in which humanity is the pinnacle of God's creation.

A quotation from Ecclesiastes integrated into the prayer reminds us (*à la* Darwin) that in the scale of things we are merely another part of the animal kingdom. Our assumed 'superiority . . . over the beasts' is worthless, empty, *hevel*. As the next verse in Ecclesiastes (unquoted in the prayer) goes on to say, both humanity and the animal world 'go to the same place: both come from the dust and both return to dust' (3:19–20). Death: the great leveller.

'Everything is vanity/emptiness, except the pure soul.' This is what the text leaves us with: the soul. Ours to value, to work on, to work with. A sort of spiritual logo. The equivalent of the trademark of Diesel, the global purveyors of jeanswear. Diesel: 'for successful living'. But doesn't successful living require work on our souls, rather than the acquisition of another pair of jeans?

Having a soul implies that although we are creatures of flesh and blood, we can think about ourselves and each other in ways that are both dispassionate and generous. We can affect the world through the choices we make, so that before we die and our bones turn to dust the world has become a somewhat better place because we have lived in it. This is no small thing. It is a vision both grandiose and humble. It refutes vanity because it dissolves our underlying self-contempt. We have a purpose: to leave the world enhanced because we have lived and suffered and struggled within it.

Work

Your work is to discover your work and then with all your heart to give yourself to it

Gautama Buddha

What a piece of work is man . . .

Hamlet, Act 2, Scene 2

Avodah

A story is told about the Maggid of Dubnow, the eighteenth-century itinerant preacher, who was asked by Rabbi Elijah ben Solomon for help in understanding his faults. Known as the Vilna Gaon (the 'Sage' of Vilna), Elijah was the greatest religious authority of the age, a master of the entire range of rabbinical literature and a student too of mathematics and sciences. Although he refused to take up the communal office of Rabbi of Vilna, he was consulted by rabbis from throughout Europe, drawn to him for his encyclopaedic knowledge and his reputation for sane and critical thinking.

At first the Maggid refused the Gaon's request. But when the Gaon persisted, he eventually spoke: 'It is known by all that you are the most pious man of our age. You study day

176

and night, retired from the world, surrounded by your books, the holy Torah, the faces of your devotees. You have reached the height of holiness. But how have you achieved it? Go down to the market place with the rest of the Jews. Endure their work, their strains, their distractions. Mingle in the world, hear the scepticism they hear, experience the everyday trials and tribulations of the ordinary man and woman in the street. Let us see then if you will remain the Vilna Gaon.' They say the Gaon broke down and wept.

Spirituality is not separate from everyday life. This is one of the underlying themes of this book. We can work at the spiritual dimension of existence within the immediate context of the daily work we find ourselves doing. Whether we're studying for exams or studying the financial pages, whether we're a potter at the wheel or pottering in the garden, whether we're unemployed or a workaholic, whether we travel the world or work from home – our sense of ourselves is (for better or worse) inextricably bound up with what we do, what we achieve, the satisfactions and dissatisfactions of our working lives. Whether our work is voluntary or paid, underpaid or overpaid, work is one of the two major sources of our sense of well-being (the other is love and relationships).

How can we develop a spirituality of work? What is required for us to experience work as a setting within which the mundanity, the tedium, the repetitiousness of work can give way – from time to time – to something else, some other way of being, some self-forgetful attentiveness where we and our work are one? Where something is working through us. Where the work in which we are engaged ceases to be labour, drudgery, hardship, burden, servitude – *avodah* in Hebrew – but is revealed as service, dedication, devotion, vocation, worship: also *avodah* in Hebrew. The biblical world view caught a glimpse of the mystery at work in work: that our way of being with it, moment by moment, can transform what would otherwise be slavery into divine service. Our work is to discover how to work.

Renewal

I enjoy my work, most of the time. I'm fortunate in this, for in my psychotherapy practice I hear many stories from people who don't: for whom work is uninspiring or stressful or just plain exhausting. But sometimes I too grow tired. Sometimes the quality of my 'being with' others is less than I would wish. Sometimes my capacity to attend to what is being said – and perhaps to hear what is not being said – becomes dulled. Usually this is when I'm trying too hard. When I allow accumulated knowledge, ideas, expectations, pressures or hopes to block my efforts to be present in the here and now of a conversation.

But over the years I've found that by emptying myself of my preoccupations – through reminding myself that meeting another is a mode of 'being' rather than of 'doing' (though the distinction is too simplistic) – something can sometimes be freed up: in me, and then mysteriously (for how does it work?) in the other. So: when I'm able to work with my impulse to work too hard, I'm more able to work together with the other person. And what we might often be working on is what might be blocking them working more effectively with me on what might be blocking them working more effectively within themselves or with others. 'What a piece of work' we are, in truth: 'how infinite in faculty . . .'

In the early years of my professional working life, when I was employed as a rabbi, my days were filled with rather frenetic activity. An endless round of meetings, pastoral visits, sermon-writing, report-writing, phone calls, administration. And then in the evening I would often have to go to a stranger's house to lead prayers. A house of mourning where a family was 'sitting *shiva*' after the death of a relative.

178

I knew there would be many mixed and powerful emotions there; and that as the rabbi I would be called upon to relate to all the sadness, the guilt, the relief, the grief, all the distressed or angry questions of life's meaning and God's purpose and the brutality of endings, and the unfairness and burden of lives lived without certainty or clarity about what it's all about. Years spent working for security, for dignity, and it comes to this: the grave, the shroud, and our little lives rounded with a sleep.

These occasions invariably brought into being a host of questions and feelings which could overwhelm me with their unarticulated demandingness, their pain and sorrow and need to make sense of what had happened: 'What does a person gain for all the toil they have expended?' (Ecclesiastes 4:9). And so I would drive through the darkness holding these thoughts at bay. There was often rain or fog or snow. Cocooned in my car I would appreciate the security of this womb, its warmth and silence. Sometimes I would listen to one of my tapes: the Beatles, Bob Dylan, Bruce Springsteen, Jefferson Airplane. (This dates me.) I would wonder if I should be listening to this on my way to a *shiva*.

It's been a long day. I've worked hard. I'm feeling exhausted. Empty. I have nothing left to give. Enough, already. 'God, this is your work . . . I don't need it, don't want it . . . If you want me to do it you'll have to give me something . . . because I've got nothing . . .' This is not my theology. It's the regressed meanderings of a tired man. Otherwise known as prayer. A prayer from a rabbi who doesn't believe in that kind of prayer.

I arrive at the house. I get out of the car. All I know is: 'You will be given what you need.' Which is what happens. Not every time, but often enough to know that whether it is an inner resource or an outer gift, some animating energy enables us to be with what unfolds, moment by moment. We may or may not be able to attune to, or encounter, this quiet strength of being – but it is present and it is real. There is something at work within us, between us, around us which the wisdom of old called by a myriad names. There is a place of renewal which is *Adonai*: the One which was, is, will be.

The Psalmist captured this spirit at the end of Psalm 90: 'May the favour of the Eternal be upon us: to support us in the work we do, and support the work we do.' The words are both a plea and a celebration. Set against our helplessness, there is the hope (and promise) that something holds us through our work, as we work.

And so, in the house of mourning the words of prayer are spoken. And there are tears. And there is silence. And a kind of catharsis occurs. Amid the disquiet of grief there is stillness and moments of eternity. Life facing death. Then there is release, and the beginning of renewal for those who mourn. Something is working its way through. We are back into the world: the cups of tea, the edgy bonhomie, the workaday concerns; and for me the drive home. Or the next meeting.

Small steps

The work is never done. The Talmud, acknowledging this, records Rabbi Tarfon's maxim: 'It is not your duty to finish the work, but nor are you free to neglect it.' This shrewd pragmatism recognises that there are limits to what we can do. It counters our guilt about not doing enough and our omnipotence that tells us we can always do more. But it balances this with the reminder that although we can allow ourselves time for relaxation and reflection and pleasure, 'the work' is what we are here to do.

Tarfon is not talking merely about the jobs we do. He is also speaking about spiritual work, religious work: in his eyes the purpose of all human activity is 'building the kingdom of God'. This is not about religious behaviourism or ritual. For rabbinic Judaism the essence of our 'work' is the reparation and amelioration of the world's discontents. The transformation of what is into what ought to be. Spiritual work involves the interpersonal, the social and the political realms of human life. We may not be able to change the world but we're not free to neglect the world as a place which needs to change – and which needs our own contribution to a process that has no end.

This contribution can take place in the smallest of interactions. Sometimes at home or at work a smile, a quiet word, a hand on an arm is the 'work' we need to do at that moment. Or our 'work' may be a generous gesture: giving money to a charity, helping someone in difficulty, buying environmentally friendly products. A myriad daily acts which change the world. This may sound like sentimentality but we have become ill-equipped to distinguish between our emotionality and the integrity of our human caring and concern.

Fulfilled existence

Sometimes our contribution may be on a larger scale. Our jobs may involve major responsibilities. Our work might affect multitudes – whether we know them or not doesn't matter. What matters is what we bring to the work: selves which recognise that our jobs are not solely of significance as a means for paying the bills or gaining financial security, or as opportunities for enhancing our careers or our self-respect, but that our work is an opening into a form of service which is integral to our spiritual development as human beings.

In a secular society divine service comes in many guises. Martin Buber describes how the founder of Hasidism, the Baal Shem Tov, taught that

> no encounter with a being or a thing in the course of our life lacks a hidden significance. The people we live with or meet with, the animals that help us . . . the soil we till, the materials

181

we shape, the tools we use, they all contain a mysterious spiritual substance . . . if we neglect this spiritual substance sent across our path, if we think only in terms of momentary purposes, without developing a genuine relationship to the beings and things in whose life we ought to take part, as they in ours, then we shall be debarred from true fulfilled existence.

This was a revolution in the understanding of spiritual work. And the spirituality of work. Through our work, and our attitude to our work, the transformation of self and society is effected.

Amid the demands and competitiveness of the world, the dictum of the ancient rabbis of Yavneh comes as a reminder and a hope: 'One may do much or one may do little. It is all one – provided one direct one's heart to heaven.' In other words our inner attitude to our actions and our work is more important than the degree of industriousness we demonstrate. If we direct our attention, moment by moment, to the opportunities that present themselves to us, the work that we do can be transformed from servitude to service, from drudgery to devotion, from hardship to worship. The secret of work is attentiveness.

Xenophobia

We must stop thinking in collective passions and
try to concentrate instead on transcendental values,
universally applicable to all peoples.

Edward Said, Palestinian-American writer

All I have is a voice
To undo the folded lie

Adrienne Rich, poet

'Thinking with the blood'

Xenophobia – a morbid dread or dislike of foreigners – has
existed for millennia. Although the word is comparatively
modern – it first appeared in 1912, preceded three years
earlier by 'xenophoby' – the condition it describes has
haunted *homo sapiens* since humanity gathered itself into
tribal groupings. This visceral 'thinking with the blood'
(Rudyard Kipling) seems hard-wired into us. Why is it that
we only seem to know who 'we' are when we can find (or
imagine) a 'them' to be opposed to?

In the biblical narrative of Cain and Abel we have a mythic
portrait of how this spiritually debilitating drama has been

present in the human family from its primitive beginnings. The story describes how 'Abel was a keeper of sheep and Cain was a worker of the ground' (Genesis 4:2). The difficulty in living with this difference lies at the root of Cain's discontent. As the brothers move warily around each other, watching each other's every move, no words pass between them until, in the absence of dialogue, a murder takes place. This seems to be the choice – either there is conversation within the human family, or another voice breaks the silence: 'the voice of your brother's blood crying from the ground' (4:10).

The 'brotherhood of man'? A fine idea, a noble aspiration. But it cannot hide the murderous hatred in the heart of men and women who fail to transcend the innate human struggle for survival and recognition, and learn to appreciate that human differences are not a threat to our existence. Sibling rivalry: the earliest form of xenophobia. The foreigner is always closer to us than we wish to acknowledge.

The Polish writer Ryszard Kapuscinski has spent his life travelling in Asia, Africa and South America, and describing in humane and dispassionate detail the vagaries, delusions and frailties of those he has encountered, from despots and dictators to those who eke out a living from the earth we share. One theme which constantly emerges is the guises in which xenophobia appear – in particular the soul-tainting stains of nationalism, racism and religious fundamentalism:

> Anyone stricken with one of these plagues is beyond reason. In his head burns a sacred pyre that awaits only its sacrificial victims. Every attempt at calm conversation will fail. He doesn't want a conversation, but a declaration . . . They are not beset by worries about the complexity of the world or about the fact that human destiny is uncertain and fragile. The anxiety that usually accompanies such questions as: What is truth? What is good? What is justice? is alien to them. They do not know the burden that weighs on those who ask them-

selves, But am I right? . . . Their world is simple – on one side we, the good people, on the other they, our enemies.

Imperium

As I was writing this chapter Jean-Marie Le Pen's anti-immigrant stance secured him an unforeseen victory in the first round of the French presidential elections. But why France should have been shocked is a mystery. A sea-change in European consciousness has seen the new century open with right-wing advances in Austria, Italy, Denmark, Holland and Belgium. Throughout the continent, the immigrant, the foreigner, the asylum seeker are soft targets for men and women fearful for their futures in a world transforming itself before our bewildered eyes. Embracing the fantasy of a fabricated national, racial or religious identity – and then defending it against outsiders – offers a pseudo-security to those who feel destabilised by the economic, social and spiritual insecurities of contemporary life.

But of course xenophobia is not merely a European phenomenon. From Jewish proto-fascists who seek to expel Palestinians from their land, to Palestinian suicide-bombers who seek the extirpation of Jews; from American neo-Nazi white supremacist rhetoric to President Bush's 'axis of evil' and the imprisonment without trial of innocent Arab-Americans; from Hindu militant fanaticism against Muslims in India, to Zimbabwe's murderous campaign of anti-white vigilantism, to the adoption in parts of the Islamic world, and Russia, and Japan, of the crudest anti-Semitic propaganda . . . we know that the list is endless. And universal. And that in each generation one could compile a similar catalogue of fear and hatred and despair. Family dramas recapitulated on a collective scale: driven by anger, blind to particularities, ignoring whatever facts seem inconvenient. Helpless in the face of the curse of Cain branded into our psyches, humanity suffers the tragic, soul-corrupting inability to tolerate difference.

Blood libel

In the early 1990s a British journalist in Bosnia spoke to
Serbian women in a village from which the local Serb militia
had removed the Muslims who had lived there for generations. What did they feel, she asked, about their Muslim
neighbours being taken away? The women thought there
was nothing to explain. Didn't she know that the Muslims
crucified Christian children, decapitated them and sent the
corpses floating down the river?

When the commander of the militia was asked why it was
necessary to 'cleanse' the area of Muslims, he replied, as if
it were a fact beyond necessary proof, that Muslims 'kill
Serbian babies and drown them in the river Drina. They
sexually assault Serbian children aged between 9 and 12 and
they cut off Serbian men's penises.'

One recognises these fantasies. In 1144 the Jewish community of the city of Norwich were accused of having
tortured and killed a Christian child in order to obtain blood
for use in Passover rituals. Within a century the blood libel
had spread, virus-like, to France, Spain and Germany. By the
eighteenth century it was widespread throughout Central
and Eastern Europe. In vain did Jews plead that their holy
books explicitly forbade the consumption of human or even
animal blood. The demonising and dehumanising function
of the blood libel can be traced through the centuries into
modern times: Julius Streicher's *Der Stürmer* frequently
devoted itself to the so-called Jewish 'murderplan'.

The Holocaust should have shattered progressive opinion's
belief in the narrative of human progress from supposedly
'primitive' ideas to increasingly rational and enlightened
thinking. But it didn't. After 1945 Europeans thought that
such structures of xenophobic fantasy as the blood libel were
disgraced for ever. Yet within a generation or so, the most
vicious myth in Europe was transferred in Serbian villages
from the Jews to the Muslims.

Victims and persecutors

It is too easy to be scornful of the absurdities in these primitive fantasies. But in treating them with the contempt they deserve we unwittingly run the risk of seeing ourselves as quite different: sensible, tolerant souls who could never think in such barbaric or unsophisticated ways. Psychoanalytic theory, however, suggests that these allegedly 'primitive' ways of thinking are a normative part of the substructure of how we all think and feel. Of course we wish to deny and disown this. Within the human psyche, though, a terrifying battle is waged, from our earliest days, between our creative, life-enhancing capacities and our destructive and death-dealing potentialities (see chapters on Creativity and Uncertainty).

For at some stage in our personal history we have all been victims. As babies, youngsters, adolescents we may be on the receiving end of verbal or physical aggression. We may have experienced some form of rejection, humiliation, abandonment. We have felt alone, frightened, neglected, trapped, taunted, or abused. The victim of someone we experienced as having more power than us or authority and control over us: a parent or sibling, or perhaps a neighbour, a schoolmate or a stranger. These experiences and memories are still inside us, alive and potent, whether we are consciously aware of them or not. We have also survived these experiences, more or less.

We had other experiences which softened the harshness. And we also found ways of sealing off from consciousness the pain of what we were going through. We discovered ways of imaging a future different from the past. We projected hope into the future so that we wouldn't feel the victim of circumstances but the author of our own lives. But that move from powerlessness to self-directing autonomy contains a psychological and spiritual danger. The depth psychologist C. G. Jung summarised it thus: 'It is the persecuted ones who persecute.' As we move towards autonomy, the feelings that went with our 'victimhood' – rage, anger, the wish to punish or destroy or gain revenge, the wish to let others feel the pain we have experienced – accompany us. And if we remain unconscious of these impulses we will be compelled to act them out. We become – in thought and sometimes in action – the persecutors.

So the potential to be a conquistador, a Stalinist, a Nazi, a xenophobe, exists within us all. We deny it at our peril. Our spiritual task includes discovering the ways in which the failure to recognise our own aggressive fantasies – our greed and lust and possessiveness, our murderousness, our wish to dominate or get attention – leads to them being projected outside of ourselves on to others, whom we will then feel are threatening us with these very same things.

Those pious Serbs were projecting their own destructiveness on to their Muslim neighbours. They could then see them annihilated, without guilt, because those others were now felt to contain all the disowned bad and destructive qualities. There are always individuals or groups available for projections: 'greedy' Jews, 'fanatical' Muslims, 'self-righteous' Christians, 'dirty' gypsies, 'immoral' gays, 'scrounging' immigrants, 'evil' empires. The projection of unacceptable parts of ourselves dehumanises others and diminishes and dehumanises ourselves.

Breaking the chain

Time and again humanity seems compelled to repeat its predisposition towards intolerance, fanaticism, xenophobia. Groups who have experienced oppression in the past find themselves acting out on the next generation the pain they've experienced. As Freud recognised, we re-enact in the present unresolved pain from the past, trying unconsciously to master it in a new situation. But in doing so we defend ourselves against 'dangers' which usually no longer exist in reality. And religious groups are complicit in this.

It's ironical that Judaism, Islam and Christianity trace themselves back to Abraham. For the biblical tradition describes Abraham's revolutionary perception that *the chain of oppression can be broken*. The compulsion towards repetition in history is not inevitable. In the story of the binding of Isaac (Genesis 22), Abraham is about to do what parents of every generation have done: to express in one form or another their aggressive fantasies towards their children. The knife is raised and he is about to sacrifice the future because of the ideology of the past: that the gods wish for human sacrifice.

But the myth dramatises the recognition that the real voice of God does not want this. The heightened awareness that makes it possible for Abraham to see that the chain of pain and oppression can be broken is what the Judaic tradition called *Adonai*: the One who is. The tragedy of religious history is that we have identified with the force that tempts Abraham to offer up his child (22:1), rather than internalising Abraham's new understanding (22:11–12) that 'God' is the energy that makes possible the transformation of 'what has always been' into what ought to be.

The danger is that a religious system of belief posited on one supreme being runs the risk of becoming fascistic. Whatever the loving and compassionate qualities attributed to 'God', one God means one God *and no others*. All other gods have to be eliminated. Humanity must 'cleanse' other gods from their minds. The temptation for the religious believer is to model themselves on this xenophobic divine being who cannot tolerate competitors.

What does it do to us psychologically and spiritually to revere a God who wishes to be the only One? God may love humanity, but he hates other gods. How often does this psychotic split become part of ourselves and our religious systems? If we are honest we know very well that all religious ideologies contain within themselves the seeds of intolerance, fanaticism and hatred. All of them can, and do, murder in the name of a loving God.

Religious adherents or devout secularists, we are all Cain's children. And our history is a nightmare from which we struggle to awake.

You

A photograph comes as a kind of reproof to the grandiosity of consciousness. Oh. So there 'I' am.

Susan Sontag, writer

Know ye not . . . that the spirit of God dwelleth within you?

1 Corinthians 3:16

Where are you?

We are nearing the end of the journey. Although the journey has no end. We have travelled from the awe and wonder at being alive in this prolific universe, through to its shadow side: the xenophobic fear and dread that within all that profusion of being we might lose track of our own individuality and aliveness and sense of purpose. As we approach the end-which-is-no-end we find ourselves spiralling back to the beginning, back to ourselves, whom we never left. Where are we? Where are *you*, the unique being reading this book?

This question is the first question the biblical story asks. The question enters paradise, the Garden of Eden, in the guise of a voice calling to Adam and to Eve. The mythic couple are hiding from the presence of the divine and they hear a question which resonates through time into the here and now of our own situation: 'Where are you?' (Genesis 3:9). The purpose of the question is not to elicit information. As Martin Buber puts it: 'God does not expect to learn something he does not know.' The purpose of the question 'is to produce an effect in man which can only be produced by just such a question, provided that it reaches man's heart – that man allows it to reach his heart'.

What Buber intuits is that the biblical storytellers implanted in their narrative an existential question addressed to anyone who is prepared to engage wholeheartedly with the myth. The characters are shown hiding: that is, avoiding responsibility for their lives. 'Where are you?' is the question which summons us to find a way of being in paradise now. This means calling ourselves to account, refusing to hide who we are, refusing to hide from ourselves.

The myth suggests that it is our failure to respond to this question truthfully which leads us to be exiled from paradise. Humanity didn't have to leave the Garden because of their appetites and desires, but because we failed to speak about them with integrity. Learning to live with this question, in all its wondrous and frightening complexity, can help us to taste paradise again. We don't have to have all the answers. But the question 'Where are you?' calls us to reflect on how we have become who we are, what our failures have been, where our achievements lie. It asks us to consider our souls and our purpose here on earth.

Two pockets

Buber records a wonderful Hasidic teaching: 'Everyone must have two pockets, so that each of us can reach into the one or the other, according to our needs. In the right pocket is to be a piece of paper with the words "For my sake was the world created", and in the left pocket a piece of paper saying "I am dust and ashes".'

We intuitively know what this is about. There are times we go along quite cheerfully, thinking we're doing pretty well in life: we're fairly good people, responsible citizens, we support the right causes, we're fair-minded and honest (after a fashion), sensitive and decent (after a fashion), tolerant (but there are limits), reasonably charitable, we try to be kind to children and animals and those less fortunate than ourselves. Life is good to us, on the whole. And haven't we, after all, worked hard for what we've achieved? Don't we deserve the rewards?

In the midst of this pleasure, this sense of well-being about our lives, our sense that we are, in spite of our limitations, something of a success as human beings – this is when we need (though we might resist it) that piece of paper in our left pocket: 'I am dust and ashes'. In the midst of our pride and self-congratulation (which can turn into grandiosity) we recall our fragility, our mortality, our insignificance in the scheme of things. Ashes to ashes, dust to dust.

As the Psalmist plangently reminds us:

Frail man, his days are like grass,
He blossoms like a flower in the field;
But the breeze passes over it and it is gone
And its place knows it no more.

Psalm 103:15–16

This is you. And me. Our days are like grass. To remember that 'I am dust and ashes' isn't about despair. It's about humility. It brings us back to a sense of our transience, that all of life is provisional, a temporary, precarious holding on, holding our breath, fending off the inevitable. Holding our breath because our breath is our life, and it is so precious. And our breath, our *ruach*, is the outer manifestation of our spirit, our soul, intangible, uncapturable, always present, always elusive, the spirit of God, the *ruach elohim* that hovered over the face of the waters at the creation of the world, the same *ruach* which is in our breathing. We are linked to the eternal. Yet one day, for us, it will stop. We will die. We are dust and ashes. This is one reality.

And the other pocket? 'For my sake was the world created'. This is not enjoining selfishness. Nor is it the three-year-old who has a tantrum because they are realising – painfully, tragically – that indeed the whole world does not revolve around them. We don't need Hasidic sayings to teach us how to be egocentric or narcissistic. That comes only too easily. 'For my sake was the world created' is about recognising one's own importance, one's own significance in the scheme of things.

This pocket reminds us that there has never been anyone like us ever before. Within all of human history, we are unique. Amid the billions of inhabitants of this planet, we are special. And this is a source of awe and wonder. When we are feeling low or dispirited or hopeless, or that life has little meaning – we reach into this right pocket and read 'For my sake was the world created'. We have a purpose here. Each of us has a purpose. What is it? What is your purpose? For your sake the world was created.

'Where are you?' What is your purpose? No one else can answer for you.

You are nothing, dust and ashes. And you are the epicentre of the world. As we wrestle with this extraordinary paradox, as we struggle to see who we are, struggling with our insignificance and our infinite significance, treading that tightrope suspended between meaninglessness and the meaningfulness of our lives, we come close to the mystery of being. We come close to the mystery of the One which accompanies our journey in this vale of tears we call our world.

Elohim

Throughout this book I have alluded to the One who is, *Adonai*, being-and-becoming. That enigmatic presence threaded through the Hebrew Bible, the texts of Jewish tradition, and the consciousness of a people wandering through time in search of a paradise always deferred and always present. It is one of the two primary names for God within Judaic thought. It is the name addressed in every Jewish blessing: 'Blessed are You, *Adonai*, Eternal One . . .' It speaks of the intimacy of an encounter – a hoped-for, anticipated-but-never-to-be-assumed momentary meeting. It is one manifestation of Martin Buber's 'I-Thou' relationship enacted in everyday life. We make ourselves present to the Presence which underpins our faltering journey. This is one name we give to Being.

But there is another name present in Judaic tradition. Translated as God (in the singular) it is grammatically a plural noun: *elohim*. Literally meaning 'the gods', 'the divine beings', this word contains a mini history lesson about the development of Israel's understanding of divinity. For as the consciousness of the Hebrew people developed they came to realise the limitations involved in conceiving of local, or localised, deities – gods of trees, hills, stones, winds, the sea, the skies, death, fertility, and so on. In an act of intellectual and imaginative expropriation, they took over the indigenous Canaanite gods, the old gods of nature and natural forces, and came to understand that natural forces were not fragmented and independent entities but aspects of one creative energetic force.

As they grew in their capacity to conceive of something containing, sustaining and nurturing them, so they formulated their understanding of divine power as a single Creator which contained within itself many disparate energies and potentialities. *Elohim*, the gods, became *elohim*, God. The Hebrew language, though, never lost its archaic resonances:

195

just as in an archaeological dig where beneath the ground level you can find evidence of earlier civilisations, we still hear, quite clearly, the plurality, the multiplicity, within the unity.

Yet although later Judaic thought insisted that God is one and whole and undivided and indivisible, the greater the tradition's insistence on God's unity, the more it is telling us that it has something to hide. And the more coercive it can feel. And what it is attempting to repress is the memory of God's inner fragmentation, God's origin in the gods.

But I don't think a contemporary spirituality needs to cover this up. On the contrary: it's much more spiritually creative (let alone psychologically healthy) for this to be open and conscious. Because it means that if God can be plural so can we. If God contains multitudes, so can we. If our God is undivided, monolithic, he runs the risk (as do we) of becoming totalitarian. He suppresses internal dissent. He cannot bear to hold together the differences inside himself. He cannot tolerate his own states of otherness. And then what kind of a model is that kind of God for us? We who need to learn how to tolerate our inner plurality of selves – so that we can learn to tolerate others in their differences. We who have to learn to live with many different parts of our self which don't always cohere into a smooth, integrated, undivided personality.

Salman Rushdie speaks of this kind of self-understanding:

> In the modern age, we have come to understand our own selves as composites, often contradictory, even internally incompatible. We have understood that each of us is many different people. Our younger selves differ from our older selves; we can be bold in the company of our lovers and timorous before our employers, principled when we instruct our children and corrupt when offered some secret temptation; we are serious and frivolous, loud and quiet, aggressive and easily abashed. The nineteenth-century concept of the integrated self has been

196

replaced by this jostling crowd of Is. And yet, unless we are damaged or deranged, we usually have a relatively clear sense of who we are. I agree with my many selves to call all of them 'me'.

Your story

Within the biblical story the God at the beginning of Genesis, who generates life out of the void, whose creativity involves a whole series of acts of differentiation and the balancing of one thing against another – light and darkness, earth and the waters, animals and humanity, female and male, rest and activity – this God holds in tension within itself a range of creative and destructive energies. 'God' is portrayed as holding within its being this polyphony of energies and voices and selves – and agreeing to call all of them *Elohim*: God.

So we face a mystery. You look into the mirror of being and find a polymorphous God, *elohim*. You look again and glimpse the One who is, *Adonai*. When Moses wishes to get to the heart of this mystery he asks to be told once and for all what to call the elusive presence he has just encountered. The response is an enigma: 'I am what I am ... I will be what I will be' (Exodus 3:14). 'God' will not be pinned down.

And neither will we. The biblical story of a God wrestling with multiplicity and unity allows our own spirituality room to breathe. You are just another struggling human being, holding within yourself a confusion of creative and destructive energies. And you contain the spirit of God. And your story is being written every moment of your life.

Zeno's Paradox

Ever tried. Ever failed. No matter. Try again. Fail again. Fail better.

Samuel Beckett, Worstward Ho

For all my efforts I achieved the result of that marksman who hit the bullseye, but of the target next to his.

Italo Svevo, The Confessions of Zeno

Language

As a child growing up in Manchester in the 1950s and early 60s I had, like children everywhere, my own set of heroes. A personal pantheon of contemporary heroic figures who represented – although of course the child never thinks of it in this way – ideals to which I could aspire. Three people stand out in my mind. There was Yuri Gagarin, the first man to fly into space. There was Bobby Charlton, who combined footballing prowess and power with an impeccable sense of fair play. And my third hero was someone who wrote with elegant craftsmanship for what in those days was the

Manchester Guardian, and whose *Letter from America* we listened to regularly on the radio at home: Alistair Cooke.

With the benefit of hindsight, I can see in my emotional engagement with these iconic figures an early flowering of several of my adult interests and passions: the wish to explore and understand what lies beyond our known, everyday world; the fervour for sport (and justice); and the affection for literature, for language, for words and what we can do with them. And what they can do to us.

And now, a confession. I remember having to write an English composition at primary school. I don't recall what the essay was supposed to be about, but I began it with this precocious rhetorical flourish: 'Manchester is famous for three things. Wherever you go in the world the city is known for its ship canal, its Hallé orchestra – and its rain.' Impressed by this blossoming prose style emerging from an otherwise unimpressive nine-year-old, my teacher read out the essay to the whole class. The only problem was that I'd pinched this opening straight from one of Alistair Cooke's recent broadcasts. Thus we have chapter one of 'my career as a plagiarist'.

In spite of my embarrassment, I learnt something important. That you can borrow (steal?) other people's words and make them your own. And the strange thing is that eventually these words and ideas that start off as someone else's do become your own. And sometimes they become so familiar, so comforting, so much a part of how you think about the world, you don't even realise any more that they didn't originate with you.

This linguistic cannibalism is, of course, a normal part of growing up. For how else does a child learn to talk and put experiences into words? Language, words and ideas bombard us from all sides, and always have done. We listened to our parents, older siblings, grandparents, teachers, schoolmates – and we began to copy, to ventriloquise, other people's words and match them to our emotions and actions. A

199

miraculous process this: learning to speak, to transform inchoate experience into coherent communication.

But if, in at least one sense, *all* our language is at root borrowed language, one of the consequences is that we may begin to sense, unnervingly, that a kind of gap exists between our deepest feelings and thoughts and intuitions, and our capacity to communicate to someone else, *or even to ourselves*, what is going on inside us.

And a further complication is that if the words we've learnt to use to describe our experiences have been mis-learnt or mis-taught, then we are going to be in quite a mess. If, for example, our early feelings of sadness have been met with 'He's just tired', or our anger has been responded to with 'Oh, she's hungry', or our jealousy or curiosity is called 'being naughty', then it may take us years to find a way to speak truthfully about what goes on within us. And all the time we are wondering why we feel distanced from others, or disconnected from feeling fully alive ourselves. When we use other people's language – as we all have to some of the time – to describe our own inner realities, we do risk being misunderstood, or misapprehending ourselves, or remaining trapped inside an impoverished inner world that just doesn't do justice to the depth and complexity of our lives.

And this is one of the problems about spirituality: how to find a language that doesn't misrepresent a dimension of being which is palpable and present and yet elusive and, perhaps, unnameable. How to find the words to speak of that which, in the final analysis, may be beyond words. This is one of the difficulties with which this book has wrestled. How to communicate in everyday language our spiritual sensibilities and potentiality without succumbing to too many clichés, platitudes or mystifications. Or retreating behind the second half of Wittgenstein's famous aphorism: 'What can be said at all can be said clearly; and whereof one cannot speak thereof one must be silent.'

Paradox

Zeno of Elea (*c*.490–*c*.430 BCE) was a Greek philosopher who developed a startling paradox. He argued that motion through space to an end-point – which we all accept as a given experience in our everyday lives – is logically impossible. In a race, Achilles can never catch a tortoise given a head start. While Achilles closes the initial gap, the tortoise has moved on. This creates a new gap. While Achilles closes that gap, the tortoise has moved on. And so on, to infinity. Achilles can never overtake the tortoise, for by the time he's arrived at where it was, it's already moved on.

Or take an arrow shot at a target. Zeno's paradox states that it can never reach its destination. For before it reaches its target it has to move through half the distance to the target. When it reaches that point, it still has further to go. Once it travels halfway through *that* remaining distance, it still has half that new distance to travel. And so on, to infinity. So, from one point of view, arrows can never reach their targets. (This paradox didn't help King Harold of England at the Battle of Hastings.)

Developing a spiritual perspective on life is like being involved in a race that cannot be won: as soon as we reach where we think we need to be, the goal has moved. We think we've 'understood' spirituality, or learned to be attentive, or pinned down God's will or location. But we cannot catch the fluidity of being in a net. We may have moments of insight; or stillness; or an awed appreciation of our significance (and insignificance) in the unfolding being-and-becoming of life. We may from time to time act in alignment with our divinely human potential. We may glimpse the mystery of how our lives are led at the intersection of the timeless with time. But once the moment is over, we realise that the journey is still going on and ahead lies ... what? What will life ask of us next?

Like the arrow that cannot reach its destination (though

it does), our spiritual selves are in perpetual flight. Quivering between distraction and attentiveness, we are always in flux: desiring, questing, questioning, struggling to see the point, or the way ahead. In which direction are we to aim? And what is the target? Like Jacob wrestling with his unnamed adversary (Genesis 32:25f), we struggle for life's blessing in the face of the unknown. We face a mystery. And we are a mystery. Can we develop a perspective on our lives to help us live with the mystery of being? 'Where I am, I don't know, I'll never know, in the silence you don't know, you must go on, I can't go on, I can't go on, I'll go on' (Samuel Beckett, *The Unnameable).*

Mystery

This book has proceeded by way of indirection. I have tried to resist, not always successfully, presenting myself as a 'reality instructor' (the term is Saul Bellow's): as a truth-teller, truth-seller, as someone who knows the answers. Rather than providing definitive statements about how things are, I wanted to undermine the known with questions that interest me. Questions about stuff that we all come across in everyday life. Often I have turned to writers and thinkers, past and present, both religious and secular – though the labels are problematic – to help me explore these themes. I'm grateful that I'm not alone. As our lives fall into the past, we all need a net of such affinities. The insights of others accompany us: signposts, hints, pointers on a journey we never finish, towards a destination we can never reach.

From a Czechoslovakian prison, where he was incarcerated for alleged 'subversion', Vaclav Havel wrote to his wife Olga about 'the question of the meaning of life'. For Havel – the political prisoner who became president of his country – this question 'is not a full stop at the end of life, but the beginning of a deeper experience of it. It is like a light whose source we cannot see, but in whose illumination we nevertheless live – whether we delight in its incomprehensible abundance or suffer from its incomprehensible paucity.' Being in constant touch with this paradox, this mystery, 'is what makes us genuinely human. Man is the only creature who is both a part of being (and thus a bearer of its mystery) and aware of that mystery as mystery. He is both the question and the questioner, and cannot help being so . . .'

Sometimes another person's words can illuminate our own inner landscape, and help us see what we have always felt but never known how to say for ourselves. Like a flash of lightning which illuminates a previously darkened landscape at night, revealing the contours and details of what has always been there, so we can read or hear other people's words – in a book or film, a conversation with a friend, or just a remark overheard in the street – and suddenly feel 'Yes, that's how it is for me too, though I never saw it so clear as now.'

Sometimes what helps us on our journey we stumble across in the course of our everyday lives. At other times we can reach back into the spiritual repository of previous generations. I feel thankful that as a Jew I have access to memories that are thousands of years old: insights recorded in scripture, in liturgy, in traditional texts, in stories and writings which reveal the experience of 'wrestling with God', of struggling with questions of hope and suffering and consolation and death, questions about the meaning and purpose of our lives. We call this *Torah*: teaching, instruction, direction. The Hebrew root means 'to shoot an arrow'.

Words

A final text, to listen in to with the attentiveness of the rabbis of old. 'Turn it over, and over,' they said of the *Torah*, 'for everything is in it':

If I am not wise, then why must I pretend to be? If I am lost, why must I pretend to have ready counsel for my contemporaries? But perhaps the value of communication depends on the acknowledgement of one's own limits, which, mysteriously, are also limits common to many others; and aren't these the same limits of a hundred or a thousand years ago? And when the air is filled with the clamour of analysis and conclusion, would it be entirely useless to admit you do not understand?

Czeslaw Milosz, Polish-American poet, b. 1911

'*If I am not wise . . .*' On the spiritual journey I've learnt to call into question my own wisdom, the pretence of cleverness, the words stolen to hide the poverty of my attempts to make sense of our lives.

'*If I am lost . . .*' Can we question our reliance on the spurious truisms and recycled clichés with which we protect ourselves from admitting how little we really understand? The verbiage with which we so confidently tell people how things are, how the world 'really' works, is a system of hideouts which prevent us attending to a deeper sense of the mystery that suffuses the world.

'*Perhaps the value of communication depends on the acknowledgement of one's own limits . . .*' A spirituality of everyday life may help us speak not with a grandiose sense of how much we know, but about our questions, our doubts, our insecurities, our limitations, our not being able to make all that much sense of the world or even our own lives. Will we then find we have more in common with others, past and present, than we ever realised?

'*And when the air is filled with the clamour of analysis and conclusion . . .*' The air is thick with trivial infotainment and 24–hour 'newsak', with fraudulent understanding too easily gained, with instant solutions to complex problems and age-old questions. The pseudo-enlightenment of untutored opinions and suspect certainties. The clamour of analysis and conclusion hides us from the anxiety-provoking possibility that often there are no answers, no simple formulae, no certainties true for all time. To acknowledge our limitations and uncertainties, without despair or false pride, is spiritual work. It's demanding – and yet it's demanded.

This book has only words to offer. Words and hints. Hints but not solutions. This is not out of deliberate coyness, but because hints and intuitions are all that we have. A hint reminds us that there is something more yet to be revealed, that we don't know it all, that 'knowing it all' is an illusion anyway. That 'not-knowing' may be a more valuable spiritual resource than grasping prematurely for something tangible, something to cling on to that might help us shore up our faltering sense of ourselves. Spirituality is not tangible. We cannot grasp the ineffable. Even though the ineffable is here and now.

This book has used words to point beyond words. Can they help us develop our attentiveness to the presence of *Adonai*, the eternal now, in all its fearful gloom and all its awesome glory? That is to say: can they help us towards more fullness of being? In an era when so many experience such an impoverished sense of reality – and I number myself among the legions – can we prepare the ground for the spirit to be present? A spiritual perspective is not something we can manufacture at will. But with sufficient attentiveness, playfulness, humour and goodwill, can the spiritual become a part of how we experience the world and our fragile lives within it?

We are in mid-flight. 'From a certain point onward there is no longer any turning back. That is the point that must be reached' (Franz Kafka). When will we arrive?

Sources, References and Endnotes

Awe

'To see a world in a grain of sand . . .': from *Auguries of Innocence*, which remained unpublished during Blake's lifetime (1757–1827). Russell Hoban, UK novelist (b. 1925, USA).

Bodies

'But O alas . . .': from 'The Exstasie', which remained unpublished during Donne's lifetime (1573–1631) – none of his poems were printed until two years after his death. The Talmudic tales are adapted from Hyam Maccoby, *The Day God Laughed*, London, Robson Books, 1978. They originate in *Berachot* 62a (Babylonian Talmud). The quotation from Freud (1856–1939) is referred to by Adam Phillips, *On Kissing, Tickling and Being Bored*, London, Faber & Faber, 1993, p. 125. *Tales of the Hasidim* by Martin Buber (1878–1965) are published in two volumes (*Early Masters* and *Later Masters*), New York, Schocken Books, 1948/1972. The story of the shoelaces is in the first volume, p. 107. For the quotations from Winnicott (1896–1971) cf. Adam Phillips, *Winnicott*, Fontana Modern Masters series, London, Fontana Press, 1988, pp. 78–9 and p. 163; also the essay 'Minds' in the same author's *Terrors and Experts*, London, Faber & Faber, 1995, pp. 93ff.

Creativity

Fury, by Salman Rushdie (b. 1947, Mumbai) later of London and New York, is published by London, Jonathan Cape, 2001. The quotation from Jeanette Winterson is taken from her column in *The Guardian* newspaper, 16 October 2001. Of the myriads of books on

206

learning to read biblical texts, I have found the following particularly helpful and recommend them unreservedly: Robert Alter, *The
Art of Biblical Narrative*, New York, Basic Books, 1981; Gabriel Josipo-
vici, *The Book of God*, Yale University Press, 1988. Some of the ideas
in this chapter, about the Creation narrative, were inspired by Andre
Neher, *The Exile of the Word*, Jewish Publication Society of America,
1981. The Auden quotation is from 'In Memory of W. B. Yeats'.

Dreams

The quotation from David Grossman (b.1954, Israel) comes from
an article by him in *The Guardian* newspaper, 22 October 2001, (G2,
p. 3). Sources for the Hasidic story are: Alan Unterman, *The Wisdom
of the Jewish Mystics*, London, Sheldon Press, 1976, pp. 72–3. He
records Nachman of Bratslav's version; and Martin Buber, *Hasidism
and Modern Man*, Humanities Press International, 1955/1988, pp.
163–4 tells it in the name of Simcha Bunam of Pzhysha (d. 1827).
The Adam Phillips quotation is from *Houdini's Box*, London, Faber &
Faber, 2001, p. 57. The best introduction to C. G. Jung (1875–1961)
is his *Man and His Symbols*, Aldus Books, 1964. The quotation by
Buñuel is taken from an article by the director Anthony Minghella
in *The Observer* newspaper, Review section, 28 October 2001, p. 9.

Emotions

The quotation from the UK novelist Zadie Smith (b. 1976) can be
found in *The Guardian* Saturday Review, 13 October 2001, p. 8. An
elaboration of the ideas in this chapter can be found in H. Cooper,
'Living With the Questions: Psychotherapy and the Myth of Self-
Fulfillment', in S. Brichto & R. Harries (eds.), *Two Cheers for Secu-
larism*, UK, Pilkington Press, 1998. The statistic '3 hours 41 minutes'
comes from the Broadcasters' Audience Research Board, 2000.

Food

The two quotations from Lionel Blue are from *To Heaven With Scribes
and Pharisees*, London, Darton, Longman & Todd, 1975, p. 39. For
the relationship between food and spirituality see also the following
books by Lionel Blue: *A Taste of Heaven: Adventures in Food and Faith*,

(with June Rose), London, Darton, Longman & Todd, 1977; *Kitchen Blues: Recipes for Body and Soul*, London, Victor Gollancz, 1985.

God

The Giuliani quote is taken from an interview with Harold Evans, *The Guardian*, 16 November 2001 (G2, p. 6). For a basic, systematic introduction to Jewish theology I always recommend Louis Jacobs, *A Jewish Theology*, London, Darton, Longman & Todd, 1973. (Note the '*A*', a typically modest gesture by an incomparable scholar.) My own theological thinking has been much influenced by Don Cupitt, some of whose ideas surface in this chapter. See in particular *The Sea of Faith*, London, BBC, 1984.

Humour

On the notion of jokes as 'devices for inducing intimacy' cf. Ted Cohen, *Jokes: Philosophical Thoughts on Joking Matters*, Chicago/ London, University of Chicago Press, 1999; and the review-essay based on it by Adam Phillips in *Promises, Promises*, London, Faber & Faber, 2000, pp. 347–57. Also 'The joy of sex and laughter', an interview with Adam Phillips in *Index on Censorship*, Vol. 29 no. 6, 2000. The 'rabbi and the flood' joke is adapted from Cohen, pp. 19–20 and the classic joke about Stalin is adapted from Leo Rosten, *The Joys of Yiddish*, London, Penguin, 1968, p. xxiv. The joke about the Cup final I owe to David Rose.

Illness

'What hours . . .' from Poems (1876–1889), no. 44, in W. H. Gardner (ed.) *Poems and Prose of Gerard Manley Hopkins*, Penguin, 1953/1970, p. 62. For the research on the links between prayer and health see *Southern Medical Journal*, Vol. 81 no. 7, July 1988; also *Mayo Clinic Proceedings* Vol. 76 no. 12, December 2001. My thanks to Professor Howard Jacobs for bringing these to my attention. The Oliver Sacks quote is from an interview in *The Observer* Review, p. 17, 9 December 2001.

Justice

'Do not judge . . .' Ethics of the Fathers, 2:5. 'On three things . . .' Ethics of the Fathers 1:18. The *midrash* about God's justice and mercy is from *Genesis Rabbah* 12:15 and is quoted in C. G. Montefiore & H. Loewe, *A Rabbinic Anthology*, New York, Schocken Books, 1974, p. 73.

Kabbalah

The parable of the orchard is from the Babylonian Talmud, *Hagigah* 14b – cf. Louis Jacobs, *Jewish Mystical Testimonies*, New York, Schocken Books, 1976, chapter 2. Other books which are relevant to this chapter include Martin Buber, *Hasidism and Modern Man*, Humanities Press International, 1955/1988; Lawrence Kushner, *Eyes Remade for Wonder*, Vermont, Jewish Lights Publishing, 1998; Gershom Scholem, *On the Kabbalah and its Symbolism*, New York, Schocken Books, 1969; Daniel C. Matt, *The Essential Kabbalah*, San Francisco, HarperCollins, 1995; Wayne Dosick, *Dancing with God*, San Francisco, HarperCollins, 1997.

Love

The quotation from Ian McEwan is from an article he wrote in response to 9/11 in *The Guardian*, 15 September 2001. The Adam Phillips quote is from *Promises, Promises*, London, Faber & Faber, 2000, p. 270. On the boundlessness (and impossibility) of love cf. Adam Phillips's use of Freud in *On Flirtation*, London, Faber & Faber, 1994, p. 39. The Larkin quote is the last line of 'An Arundel Tomb', from *The Whitsun Weddings*, London, Faber & Faber, 1964/1984. R. M. Rilke (b. Prague, 1875–1926). L. Boerne (1786–1837). 'Love God . . .' Babylonian Talmud, *Yoma* 86a. The quotation from Buber is from *Ten Rungs: Hasidic Sayings*, New York, Schocken Books, 1947/1970, p. 82. The Moshe Leib story is adapted from Louis Newman, *Hasidic Anthology*, New York, Schocken Books, 1972. 'Everyone is a letter . . .' (Nachman of Bratslav).

Money

The statistics quoted (from the United Nations Development Agency) are in an article by Zygmunt Bauman, *The Guardian* Saturday Review, 12 January 2002, p. 2. On the Jewish ethics of business cf. Ganzfried-Goldin (ed.), *Code of Jewish Law (Kitzur Shulchan Aruch)*, New York, Hebrew Publishing Co., 1961, Vol. 2, section 62:16, p. 38. The Deepak Chopra quote is from *The Seven Laws of Spiritual Success*, Amber-Allen Publishers, 1995.

Nothingness

John Ashbery (b. New York, 1927). Gershom Scholem (b. Berlin, 1897–1982). The quotation from Paul Valéry (1871–1945) is taken from Adam Phillips, *Terrors and Experts,* London, Faber & Faber, 1995, p. 13. Part of the background to 'Sarah's Story' is the conflict between Hagar and Sarah. When Sarah was unable to conceive, Abraham fathered a child (Ishmael) with his Egyptian maid, Hagar. The story of the resulting conflict between the two women is narrated in Genesis chapters 16 and 21. Other themes behind my contemporary *midrash* can be found in Avivah Gottleib Zornberg, *The Beginning of Desire: Reflections on Genesis*, New York/London, Image Books, Doubleday, 1995, chapter 5. And the end of the story refers to the close of Philip Roth's luminous *I Married a Communist*, London, Jonathan Cape, 1998.

Orifices

'If we picture the mind . . .' Adam Phillips, *Promises, Promises*, London, Faber & Faber, 2000, p. 161. The Nahmanides (Rabbi Moses ben Nahman 1194–1270) passage is adapted from Francine Klagsbrun, *Voices of Wisdom: Jewish Ideals and Ethics for Everyday Living*, Philadelphia, Jewish Publication Society of America, 1980, pp. 95–6. On traditional Jewish attitudes towards sexuality see Arthur Waskow, 'Down-to-Earth Judaism: Sexuality', in Jonathan Magonet (ed.), *Jewish Explorations of Sexuality*, Oxford, Berghahn Books, 1995.

Pleasure

The Zusya story is adapted from Elie Wiesel, *Souls on Fire*, London, Weidenfeld & Nicolson, 1972, p. 120. Saul Bellow, *Mr. Sammler's Planet*, Penguin Books, 1970, pp. 183–4. The quotation from Robyn Davidson is from her article in *The Guardian* Saturday Review, 2 February 2002, p. 14.

Quiet

'It is not necessary . . .', Franz Kafka (b. Prague, 1883–1924), *Shorter Works*, Vol. 1, London, Secker & Warburg, 1973, p. 102.

Relationships

'All real living . . .', from *I and Thou* (translated Ronald Gregor Smith), Collier Books, New York, Macmillan Publishing Co., 1958/1987, p. 11. The Nachman of Bratslav story is adapted from Alan Unterman, *The Wisdom of the Jewish Mystics*, London, Sheldon Press, 1976, pp. 71–2. Buber's story about his mother is extracted from Aubrey Hodes, *Encounter with Martin Buber*, Penguin Books, London, 1972, p. 55. Hodes reports this as Buber's oral account to him; Buber's own version can be found in his *Meetings*, La Salle, Illinois, Open Court Publishing Co., 1973, p. 18. *Meetings* also contains his account of his I–Thou contact with the horse, pp. 26–7. 'Existence will remain meaningless . . .', from 'The Silent Question: On Henri Bergson and Simone Weil' (1951), in what is still the best one-volume anthology of Buber's writings: Will Herberg (ed.), *The Writings of Martin Buber*, Meridian Books, New York, The World Publishing Co, 1956/1965, p. 314.

Sport

John Updike, US novelist and essayist (b. 1932). Sport seems to attract the literary talents of several of our finest prose stylists, e.g. American writers Norman Mailer, Joyce Carol Oates and Stephen Jay Gould and the UK novelist Martin Amis. Leni Riefenstahl (b. 1902), German film-maker who used her art to mythologise the Nazis. Her epic documentary of the 1936 Berlin Olympics (*Olympia*) was given a gala premier on Hitler's 49th birthday. 'Weekend Taliban' is a phrase coined by the novelist Tim Parks.

Truth

Iris Murdoch, UK novelist (1919–99). The quotation from Alfred Adler (1870–1937), a Viennese colleague of Freud, is from *The Problem of Neurosis* (1929). Friedrich Nietzsche (1844–1900) is the presiding intellectual spirit hovering over the century he did not live to see. The Oliver Sacks (b. 1933) quotation is from *Uncle Tungsten: Memories of a Chemical Boyhood*, New York, Knopf, 2002. The quotation from Kierkegaard (1813–55) is from *The Last Years, Journals 1853–1855*. The *Hamlet* quotation is Act 1, Scene 3, line 76. The Farber (1914–81) quotation is from 'Lying on the Couch' (1978), reprinted in *Salmagundi*, No. 123, Summer 1999, p. 167. Kafka's aphorism is from *Shorter Works*, Vol. 1, London, Secker & Warburg, 1973, p. 84.

Uncertainty

The story of Israel of Rizhyn (d. 1850) is told in Martin Buber, *Tales of the Hasidim (Later Masters)*, New York, Schocken Books, 1948/1972, pp. 59–60.

Vanity

For more background on the insidious culture of brands cf. Madeleine Bunting, 'The new gods', in *The Guardian*, 9 July 2001 (G2, pp. 4–5).

Work

The story of the Maggid is derived from an account narrated by US novelist Herman Wouk (b. 1915) in *This is My God*. Tarfon's aphorism is from Ethics of the Fathers 2:21. The Buber quotation is from *Hasidism and Modern Man*, Humanities Press International, 1955/1988, p. 165. The Babylonian Talmud, *Berachot* 17a, is the source for the text from the rabbis of Yavneh.

Xenophobia

The quotations from Edward Said (b. 1935, Jerusalem) and Kapuscinski are taken from *The New York Review of Books*, 3 November 1994. Adrienne Rich (b. 1929, Baltimore). The phrase 'thinking with the blood' from the British Nobel Prize-winning novelist Rudyard Kipling (b. Mumbai, 1865–1936) is quoted in Martin Amis, *Experience*, London, Vintage, 2001, p. 222, who adds (ruefully?) ' . . . instead of *about* the blood, as you ought soberly to do'. The material on Serbia derives from an article in *The Observer* newspaper during 1993 by Neal Ascherson.

You

The quotation from Susan Sontag (b. 1933, New York) is from *On Photography* (1976). The Buber quotation is from *Hasidism and Modern Man*, Humanities Press International, 1955/1988, p. 125. And the tale of the two pockets is from his *Ten Rungs: Hasidic Sayings*, New York, Schocken Books, 1947/1970, p. 106. The Rushdie quote is from an interview in *The Observer* newspaper, 10 August 1997.

Zeno's Paradox

Samuel Beckett (b. Dublin, 1906–1989): *Worstword Ho* (1983), *The Unnameable* (1959). Italo Svevo (born Ettore Schmitz in Trieste, 1861) published his *Confessions of Zeno* in 1923. He died in 1928 in a car accident. The quotation from Havel (b. Prague, 1936) is from *Granta* 21, Spring 1987, p. 227. 'Turn it over, and over . . .' is from Ethics of the Fathers 5:25. The problem with being a magpie is that sometimes one loses what one picks up: thus the quotation from Milosz remains unsourced. The Kafka aphorism is a variant translation on the version (no. 5) in *Shorter Works*, Vol. 1, London, Secker & Warburg, 1973, p. 85.

Out of respect for scholarly convention, all quotations incorporated into my text retain their original gendered language: 'he', 'man', 'mankind' etc. My own writing tries to avoid this trope.

Translations from the Bible or Jewish liturgy are my own except where indicated.